Sea Kayaking Maryland's Chesapeake Bay

Sea Kayaking Maryland's Chesapeake Bay

Day Trips on the Tidal Tributaries and Coastlines of the Western and Eastern Shore

Michael Savario and Andrea Nolan

BACKCOUNTRY GUIDES
WOODSTOCK, VERMONT

In memory of my father, James Nolan, who gave me the gift of literature, a love for the natural world, and the ability to realize my dreams. —A.N.

I would like to dedicate this book to my wife, Kristen, for all her support through the years and her appreciation of the wonder of nature. I would also like to thank all the folks at Amphibious Horizons Sea Kayaking, Ranger Dave Davis and Netta Satina with the Maryland Department of Natural Resources, and Dorcas Miller, author of *Kayaking the Maine Coast: A Paddler's Guide to Day Trips from Kittery to Cobscook.* —M.S.

ISBN 0-88150-567-6
ISSN 1547-0393

Cover and interior design by Faith Hague
Composition by Chelsea Cloeter
Cover photograph © Tadder/Baltimore
Interior photographs by the authors unless otherwise indicated
Maps by Paul Woodward, © 2003 The Countryman Press

Published by Backcountry Guides, a division of
The Countryman Press
P.O. Box 748
Woodstock, VT 05091

Distributed by W. W. Norton & Company, Inc.
500 Fifth Avenue
New York, NY 10110

Printed in the United States of America

10 9 8 7 6 5 4 3

Contents

Introduction

Maryland is a land defined by its water. A paddler's paradise, the Chesapeake Bay offers many lifetimes of kayaking opportunities as it carves a broad path through the center of this small state. Named *Chesepiooc* ("Great Shellfish Bay") by the Algonquin Indians, the Chesapeake is a fertile and rich ecosystem that is a mixture of salt and fresh water, a landscape that is tidal for its entire length. Its tributaries can change from salt to brackish to fresh water during a day's paddle. Because of this mixture, freshwater animals are found in the upper parts of the Chesapeake and its rivers, and every fish or marine mammal that swims in the Atlantic can live in the salty lower waters. The bay's tidal boundaries are elusive, influencing the region's culture and creating a unique and beautiful landscape of water and earth.

Formed by rising sea levels when the last ice age ended 12 thousand years ago, the Chesapeake Bay watershed includes parts of six states and the District of Columbia and is the drowned river valley of the Susquehanna River. It is a shallow bay, and its average depth of 21 feet would be considerably less if not for the deep channel of that ancient river. Flowing for 195 miles from the delta of the Susquehanna Flats (by Havre De Grace) to the Atlantic Ocean, the bay has a sprawling tidal shoreline of 5,600 miles: 3,200 miles of this shoreline lie in Maryland. Water is literally everywhere—on the flat coastal plain of the eastern shore you cannot walk a mile in any direction without getting your feet wet. Within this water world there is a dizzying array of paddling opportunities. Nineteen major rivers flow into the bay, as do an additional 400 minor rivers and creeks. Draining into these waters are thousands of lesser creeks, runs, streams, sloughs, guts and inlets of all widths and depths. The sea kayak, which can be paddled in rough open water and in mere inches of water, is the ideal vessel for exploring this varying landscape.

This maze of waterways is our home. We formed Amphibious Horizons Sea Kayaking in 1997 to share our love of the bay and to expose people to the unique Chesapeake landscape. We both have led environmental education canoe programs for the Chesapeake Bay Foundation. Mike continues as the owner of Amphibious Horizons, and Andrea left the company in the autumn of 2002. However, both of our hearts and souls remain lodged deep within the bay. In these descriptions we point out our favorite routes, pathways that will lead you through labyrinths of marshland, past immense rookeries of herons, and into some of the most beautiful places on earth.

The layout of this book is simple, shaped by the geography of Maryland. We have included our favorite 30 day trips. The trips are organized from south to north, along the western shore, looping over the top of the bay and continuing north to south down the eastern shore. Andrea wrote the western shore trips, looping over the top of the bay to write about the Sassafras River. Mike wrote about Perryville, at the top of the bay, and then continued down the bay, writing all of the trips from the Chester River on southward. We follow the same format: beginning with a brief description of the general attributes of the location, and follow with information about trip length and the expected mileage of the route described (paddling routes range from 5 to 26 miles). Next we describe the put-in site (and pullout site when different), providing information on fees, permit requirements, and facilities. We then give driving directions, beginning with the nearest major road (you should use a Maryland map to augment these directions). The western shore and Sassafras River directions are given from the nearest major road, the remainder of the eastern shore directions are given from Annapolis. We finish with paddling notes, where you will find the bulk of our trip description. Our style is narrative, as we hope to create for the reader the experience of having a local guide.

In the Chesapeake, no borders are distinct and so it shall be with this guidebook. We have included natural history and local knowledge, which is often placed in easily referenced information boxes. If you come upon an unfamiliar term you will usually find the definition in one of these sections. Our hope is that we placed this information so you can find it when it will be most useful—reading about cownose rays when you are surrounded by them at Wye Island, or learning about mummichogs when you have hundreds of little fish on the Sassafras River clamoring to get into your kayak.

This guide is about day trips, but it is quite possible to combine trips to create a paddling weekend or week. We have included an appendix listing resources for finding campsites, hotels, and bed & breakfasts near our trip locations. We have tried to provide information that will enrich your paddling experience, but the Chesapeake's natural and social history is so rich that a book could be written about each trip. We have included references and recommended reading so you can discover more about the bay and its tributaries.

We provide route descriptions for the inexperienced and experienced paddler, for the distance hound and the poke-boater. Thus, the waterways explored in this guidebook are both open bay and small creek; they are wide rivers and narrow guts. Except for islands, the trip routes lead the kayaker up and back down a stretch of water, eliminating the hassle of having a shuttle vehicle. Besides its ease, the main

Mike Savario

Returning to the Inn of Silent Music B&B after a day of paddling around Smith Island.

virtue of there-and-back paddling is that it emphasizes the importance of the journey over the destination, and encourages general poking about and meandering. The river is alive and in a constant state of change; the tide ebbs and flows; the quality of light changes and a river becomes transformed in the course of hours. Much of the water's beauty can only be revealed on the "back" section of your journey, when you are no longer engrossed in finding the route and have settled into the Zen of paddling.

Paddle the same waterways over and over until it feels like you are coming home whenever you slip your boat into the water. Kayak off the chart, explore new places, like a child experiencing the world for the first time. Slow down, join the pace of nature.

Sea kayaking unlocks the beauty, peace, and solitude of Maryland's Chesapeake Bay. Wander our water with no destination in mind, because as Rat pointed out to Mole in *The Wind in the Willows* "There is nothing—absolutely nothing—half as much worth doing as simply messing about in boats."

Tools and Skills

While it is our intention to integrate all information into the main text of the trip descriptions, some mention of the tools and skills needed to safely paddle the Chesapeake Bay cannot wait.

Your Kayak

The Chesapeake Bay's width and depth ranges widely. Within the course of a day trip your surrounding environment can change from a narrow gut to a 100-foot-wide creek to a 15 mile expanse of open bay. Within this varied water, the expedition sea kayak stands out as the ideal craft for the intrepid paddler. The hardy dimensions of the sea kayak were designed for rough arctic seas. It is stable and swift over great distances and on rough waters, and has a shallow draft and maneuverability that allows it to navigate the same shallow waters as our native canoe. An expedition kayak is generally a closed deck kayak, 15 to 18 feet long and 22 to 24 inches wide, with bulkheads both forward and

Mike Savario

Smith Island

aft separating the cockpit from the bow and stern sections. These dimensions may make the kayak feel unstable initially, but they actually enable the kayak to handle smoothly in rough seas. In addition, so long as the hatches stay closed in the event of capsize, they prevent the entire kayak from swamping and sinking, thus enabling you to have a floating craft making assisted rescue or self-rescue easier. The recreational kayak is generally quite wide, relatively short, with an open cockpit. These kayaks are essentially designed for poke boating. Recreational boats feel stable initially, but offer very little resistance to capsize in chop. They should never be paddled in open water subject to wind-generated waves, or in areas with powerboat traffic. When a recreational kayak does capsize or swamp it can be impossible to empty at sea. These shorter, fatter boats also have a slower hull speed, requiring much more energy from the paddler, which would make some of the longer trips in this book more difficult.

Those who feel uncomfortable in the confinement of the expedition kayak but still want to paddle all the waterways of the bay might look at many of the excellent hybrids on the market. These models pair some of the more comfortable traits of the recreational kayak, with almost the same speed and adaptability of the expedition kayak. We would still not recommend extreme, rough water or surf travel in these boats, but most are suitable for the trips we list on all but the windiest days. There are also several good sit-on-top kayaks on the market that have the same approximate dimensions of expedition kayaks and are suitable for summer, warm water kayaking. Just make sure that the sit-on-top you choose is intended for distance paddling, and not just for playing in the surf. Consult your local kayak outfitter and they will steer you in the right direction.

Gear

Once you have the right boat, you need the appropriate gear. Kayak instruction books are full of useful information on how to pack and what to bring. We highly recommend using one of these manuals as a reference for your kayaking. In brief, for a day trip, regardless of the season, we recommend:

2 paddles (one primary and one break-down spare that is stowed on deck)

1 personal flotation device (PFD) with an attached whistle (It is required by law to have this with you. We highly recommend wearing your PFD. Most drowning victims were not.)

1 spray skirt

1 paddle float

1 bilge pump

1 sponge

A chart or map of the area along with any paddling notes (These items should be laminated or stored in a waterproof, see-through bag and stashed under your forward deck bungies.)

Compass (Can be either hand held or deck mounted. You could also use a hand held, waterproof GPS unit, but when the batteries or satellite link-up fails you need to have a backup.)

Filled water bottle and at least ½ gallon of spare water, per person

Food (Kayaking is no time for fasting! Pack more lunch and snacks than normal so that you have some fuel for your fire when the paddling gets tough.)

Dry bag with spare warm clothes and rain gear (We have treated people for hypothermia in June, so bring the bag of clothes even if the day is warm. Also, expect daily afternoon squalls during the summer months.)

20 foot length of thin pea cord (for tying up to dinghy docks, or any other eventuality that may occur.)

Tow belt (While you could use the pea cord, a quick-release tow belt is safer and more efficient when towing is necessary.)

Flares (hand held and aerial) and strobe light

Flashlight (Delays happen, so bring a light even if you plan on returning by dusk.)

Extra batteries

Cell phone and/or portable VHF marine radio (You shouldn't count on these items always working—you could be out of range during some of the trips.)

First aid kit (and the knowledge to use it.)

Matches

Sunscreeen

Weather radio (VHF radio have weather channels)

Field identification book(s) for birds, plants, and animals (While it is fun to observe nature, it is more fun to know what you are seeing.)

One thing to leave behind is your paddling itinerary. Give this to a friend or relative and include information on:

- Your boat type and color
- The number and names of people in your paddling group
- Your put-in site
- Your expected route
- When you plan to be home. (Include information on who to contact if you do not return when expected.)

Some safety contact numbers are included in the appendix. Most of your trips will be uneventful, but bad things can happen. In the event of an emergency or injury, keep calm, evaluate the situation, and then formulate a solution. The power of adrenaline over rational thinking can be immense, so as long as no one in your group is in life-threatening danger, taking a minute to settle your nerves makes a world of difference. Make sure that you are familiar with your first aid kit. You may want to invest in a wilderness first aid course to augment your skills (information on these courses can be found in the appendix). Besides learning how to prevent and treat injuries, it is important to learn about environmental injuries such as hypo- and hyperthermia. We have included some information about the recognition and prevention of these conditions in Appendix B, "Preventing and Recognizing Hypothermia and Hyperthermia."

The best preparation is prevention, and the most common cause of hardship or accidents is lack of ability, preparation, and fitness. So, once you are geared up, you need to get skilled up. This book is not an instruction manual—we do not teach you how to kayak. You will find many fine books and resources in the appendix to help with that. However, we will offer a few notes on the skills needed for the trips in this guide and some tips on how to gain those skills.

Paddling Ability

You must have some basic skills to safely paddle the routes in this book. To kayak with a group of people you should be able to maneuver your boat confidently, to brace in choppy conditions, and to perform an assisted rescue and an unassisted rescue. Your risk and exposure to accident or injury is greatly increased if you paddle solo—you must have hard-wired self-rescue and paddling skills. Along with strokes and rescues, you also need to develop judgment, navigation, and group paddling skills. It is also recommended that you learn how to complete a kayak roll if your boat will enable you to do so, as the roll is the preferred self-rescue technique since you never have to leave your boat. Restrict your paddling to the many protected tidal waterways that we describe in this book while you are learning. As your skill level and confidence increase, you can gradually move onto partially open water, and then full-exposure open water trips. The Chesapeake waters can be deceivingly calm—conditions can change in an instant with summer squalls or passing squadrons of powerboats. It is always safest to paddle with two or more people, particularly in open water and definitely when making any open water crossings. There is safety in numbers when it comes to rescues, and your visibility to other boaters on the water increases dramatically as a larger group. We are the little fish out there; we need to mimic the schooling minnows.

Learning How to Kayak

Our best advice is to get professional instruction from a commercial outfitter that provides American Canoe Association or British Canoe Union certified instructors. Paid instruction is available in small groups or on an individual basis and should be primarily taught out of the classroom and on the water. The perk of professional instruction is that you are assured that all the necessary skills will be thoroughly covered and taught (see appendix for resources). You can also gain skills by joining a local paddling club like the Chesapeake Paddler's Association. The members of these organizations are usually eager to teach one another new skills and embrace novice paddlers. You can also supplement your education by purchasing one of the many excellent kayak instruction books on the market. You are ultimately responsible for your own safety, so learn, learn, learn and practice, practice, practice.

Minimum Impact Kayaking

Kayaks don't burn fossil fuels or tear up grass beds with propellers, and so are much more environmentally friendly than motorboats. However, we still occupy space and need to be responsible for how we change the natural world we are enjoying. While any one paddler's impact may not seem great, the cumulative effect of repeated visitors can be harmful if we are not careful.

Leave No Trace

The primary credo in the Leave-No-Trace ethic is simple: leave a place the same or better than you found it. Carry out *all* of your trash—even if your paper lunch bag or orange peel will decompose. Pick up other people's trash as well; some plastic bags or bottles won't take up much space under your kayak's deck bungies, and the bay will be a bit cleaner.

If you create human waste of the solid variety, plan ahead and bring a container to pack it out with you. While it may seem as if one little cat hole won't make much difference, remember that dry land spots on the Chesapeake are rare. You will not be the first or last kayaker to use a break spot. For individuals, we recommend carrying a tight sealing plastic storage container in a small dry bag along with a roll of toilet paper. You can use an inverted plastic bag to scoop up your waste, thus eliminating the need for perfect aim into the container. Feminine hygiene products can be packed out in a separate, doubled up, zip-loc bag.

Even if you remove all of your waste, your kayak can leave its mark. When possible, land on public property, beaching your kayak on sand or firm bare mud; leave the marsh grasses in peace to prevent erosion and the destruction of habitat. Be respectful of landowners. The area below the mean high-tide line is public domain, but that doesn't mean you should land in someone's backyard. If public land is lacking, there are usually plenty of farm fields with a quiet, remote shoreline. You should never land on a private pier or boat landing unless it is an emergency.

Do not get too close to the wildlife you observe, both during rest stops and while underway. It is one thing to observe osprey in their nests and another to harass them. Minimum impact applies to the entire world surrounding your kayak, so make a good name for sea kayakers whenever you travel. If you see a crab pot buoy, leave it alone. Stay clear of fishermen's lines and always obey the rule of mass tonnage: stay out of the way of boat channels and any boats that are bigger, faster, or less able to maneuver than you. Channels are generally clearly marked, with red, even-numbered, day markers or buoys lining the right side of channels when traveling upstream ("red, right, returning" is a helpful way to remember this). It takes very little effort to be a low impact kayaker. Just think of the bay as your own backyard, other boaters as friendly neighbors, and never ever pet the wildlife.

When Underway

While our trip descriptions are detailed, you will need some navigating skills to use this guide. Keep your waterproof charts and paddling notes on the deck and refer to them often. Constantly match your location to the map, and supplement our maps with nautical charts, county road map books, and topographic maps. Be comfortable using a compass and use "aids to navigation" such as channel markers to pinpoint your location and to stay clear of channels. A watch can be your best navigation tool in the tidal marshes, where channel markers and landmarks are often lacking. Know your paddling pace and use that information to keep approximate track of your location. The average paddling pace is 3 miles an hour, but this can change based on the prevailing winds, your companions, and on the purpose of your trip (distance vs. nature observation). Test your pace by timing how long it takes to kayak a well-landmarked mile and retest this rate whenever necessary (such as the wind dramatically increasing or decreasing). Remember to factor in you and your companions' fitness when planning a trip—while you may paddle at 3 miles an hour in the morning, your power may lag by mile 19.

For the well-prepared paddler the Chesapeake Bay is safe and gentle. The ever-changing gold and green boundaries of land and water will seduce and enchant the most world-traveled paddler. The Chesapeake is our home, and just as we always have room for one more at our dinner table, there will always be room for one more kayaker along our graceful shores. Happy paddling.

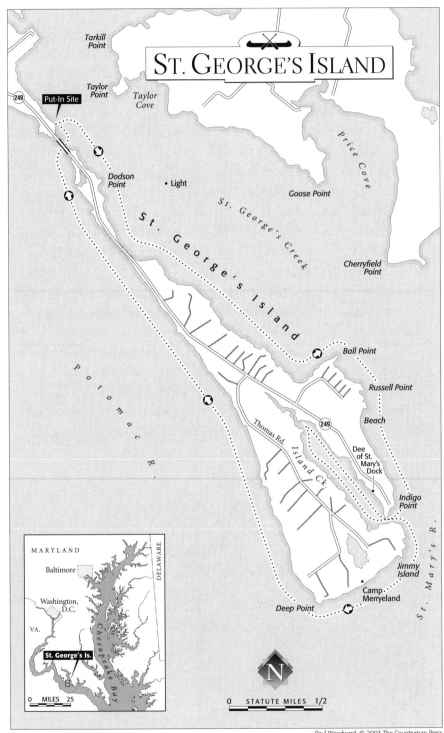

ST. GEORGE'S ISLAND

Tarkill
Point

Taylor
Point

Taylor
Cove

249

Put-In Site

Price Cove

Dodson
Point

Light

Goose Point

St. George's Creek

St. George's Island

Cherryfield
Point

Ball Point

Russell Point

Potomac R.

Beach

249

Thomas Rd.

Island Ck.

Dee
of St.
Mary's
Dock

Indigo
Point

St. Mary's R.

Jimmy
Island

Camp
Merryeland

Deep Point

MARYLAND

Baltimore

DELAWARE

Washington,
D.C.

VA.

Chesapeake Bay

St. George's Is.

0   MILES   25

N

0   STATUTE MILES   1/2

Paul Woodward, © 2003 The Countryman Press

Part I

Western Shore

1. St. George's Island

Length: At 9 miles, including a detour up Island Creek, St. George's is the perfect length for an unhurried easy day's trip for any level paddler. For more advanced paddlers there is plenty of water upstream (St. George's Creek) to explore once your circumnavigation is done.

Put-in Site: A public landing is located just before the bridge onto St. George's. There are port-a-john's at this boat landing and there is no fee for launching. It is a concrete ramp for powerboats, but I have never found the place too busy, even on the most beautiful of Saturdays.

Andrea Nolan

Osprey

Driving Directions: MD 5 South is accessible from exit 7A on I-495 or from US 301, which joins with MD 5 for about 4 miles (in Waldorf) until MD 5 branches off to the south. Follow MD 5 south for about 42 miles (from 301) until you take a right at a traffic light onto MD 249. Follow 249 until it ends at St. George's Island in 11 miles. The boat landing is on the left before the bridge.

ST. GEORGE'S ISLAND is a waterman's hamlet on a delicate sliver of land at the end of a small peninsula 10 miles northwest of the mouth the Potomac. While little more than 6 miles in circumference, the island makes the most of its mileage: it is nearly bisected by its own creek and is bordered by two rivers, a creek, and an inlet. St. George's Creek creates the upper northeast boundary, then is overpowered by the St. Mary's River for the lower northeast section. The southern tip and southwestern border of the island face the broad Potomac, with the opposite shoreline a distant 5 miles and a state away. It is very nearly the furthest you can live in the state without becoming a Virginian. This is an old community established before the Revolutionary War. St. George's Islanders fought the first Maryland battle of that war for independence, disabling five British warships in the process. The community's roots have changed little over the years and it remains an island deeply tied to the water, home to many waterman and seafood packing houses. Although small in size, this island leaves a vivid imprint on any kayaker who paddles by its pine-covered shoreline, bristling with piers and fishing nets.

Paddling Notes

Since this is a circumnavigation, you could paddle either direction around the island. I always paddle the island in a clockwise direction, since I prefer the closer shorelines and more leeward feel of those waters in the lazy morning hours. However, paddling on the Potomac can work as well, and could be a good option if strong winds are predicted for later in the day. Most of our winds and storms come from the west, so if weather does arrive you would be better protected on the sheltered northeastern side of the island. One afternoon my group was caught in a squall on the Potomac side of the island and while we were drenched in seconds, we had a great time watching the storm sweep in over the open water. It is all a matter of perspective and preparedness.

To paddle the northeastern side of the island, do not cross under the bridge; just parallel it southeast as you make the short crossing to the island, then keep the island to your right and you cannot go wrong. For the first mile, St. George's is quite narrow and the water is shallow, with an average depth of 3 feet. There are dense beds of submerged aquatic vegetation (SAVs) growing here and thus it is not uncommon to see swans in this area. This section of the island is generally composed of small homes and piers. After the first mile the shoreline begins to swing out as the island broadens. In ¼ mile you will round Ball Point and the island will resume its southeast orientation. Your trip began on St. George's Creek, but after Ball Point you are on the mighty St. Mary's River and you will notice that the eastern shoreline is much farther away. In another ¼ mile you will round Russell Point and the island begins to narrow again. The final mile-long stretch of island is wild saltwater marsh, dominated by black needle rush and cordgrass, with narrow sandy beaches lining the water. This length of paradise ends at Indigo Point, which is the tip of the island and one side of the mouth of Island Creek.

You will have to swing your kayak out away from the island to get around the breakwater that protects the channel of Island Creek. On your way into the Creek make sure you give way to any passing powerboats. Although the boats are generally shallow-drafted workboats, they still have less maneuvering room in the channel than a kayaker. Island Creek is a calm little oasis, and the water will be quite flat even on the windiest of days. Shortly after you enter the creek you may see the *Dee of St. Mary's* to your right, which is a skipjack owned by Jack Russell and operated as a living classroom for any group who wishes to charter a trip. I have been lucky enough to go on several great trips with Captain Jack. Participants get to help raise the massive sail, haul an oyster dreg and are treated to informative stories of Chesapeake life by the captain himself. (Call 301-994-2245 or visit www.skipjacktours.com for more

Osprey

Everywhere you paddle in the bay you will see the cocky osprey, with its distinctly mottled white head and underbelly, and brown mask and back. They fly much closer to the water than bald eagles and are also easily spotted while sitting on the nesting platforms which punctuate the bay. As you approach a nest, their mate is usually perched only yards away, eyeing you warily as you near its family. If you get too close the osprey will swoop down on you, sending the unmistakable message to back off while allowing you a close look at its distinctly pointed and backswept wings. Thirty years ago, the Chesapeake's osprey population was severely decimated by pesticide poisoning and habitat loss. Their triumphant return is due to the banning of DDT and the construction of thousands of osprey platforms to replace their preferred natural habitat of dead trees. It was a simple problem with simple solutions, making the osprey a conservation success story.

The osprey's local name—fish hawk—is appropriate because unlike the carrion-eating bald eagle, osprey are more exclusive in their eating habits. They dine only on live fish and are skilled hunters, hovering 100 feet over the water to spot their prey and then usually dropping in steps toward the water before entering a full dive. When hitting their target, osprey swing their legs down and forward, sometimes striking the water with such a force that they submerge but, more commonly, just dunking their talons before flying away with a fish in their grip, which they deftly flip so that it is in the best aerodynamic position for flight.

information.)

Take the time to paddle in the still air up to the head of Island Creek, where you can pass some easy time watching the great blue herons and snowy egrets stalking the shallows for killifish and silversides. There are numerous osprey nests in the creek, along with one low nesting platform near the headwaters that was built only a few feet above the water. In the afternoon you will often see a couple of diesel workboats docked in the creek's protective waters after a morning of fishing. Their low sides and gentle lines are as native to this water as the osprey.

Once you finish exploring the creek, paddle to the right from the mouth and you will find yourself at the flat tip of the island that is wholly comprised of Camp Merryelande's vacation cottages. The brightly painted buildings strung along the shoreline always give me the

Osprey are monogamous, with both sexes equally sharing nest preparation, egg incubation, chick watching, and food gathering. If you pass a nest and the parent bird rises on its legs and chirps like a loud canary, then it is a protecting and incubating unhatched eggs. If the parent rises and hovers in flight above the nest, sometimes swooping down and dragging its talons in the water, then the eggs have hatched and there are chicks in the nest, usually two or three. If you get close enough to elicit either the deranged canary chirp or a flight from the nest than you are too close. Personal boundaries vary from osprey to osprey.

After living in monogamous bliss together from March through September, our Chesapeake osprey leave to winter in Central and South America, the males and the females separating for the entire season. Every year around St. Patrick's Day they return to their same nest site, often reuniting on the same day each year. They lay their eggs in May, after patching up their nest and consummating their reunion. The osprey does not get nearly as much respect or acclaim as the bald eagle, but it should. It is a fierce predator and defender of its young, and is so swift when flying that it can make a bald eagle seem like a lumbering giant. They will chase one another, bald eagles, and heron, but for all of their bullying and bravado, osprey rarely steal prey and are more often the victim of fish thievery. I wait for the return of my favorite aerial acrobat every March to assure me that the warm days of spring are soon to come. *—A.N.*

feeling that I took a wrong turn and landed in Key West. Along with the cottages, there are RV and tent sites in the pinewoods, making Camp Merryelande an excellent place to base a week or a weekend of paddling. Even if you are not staying at the camp, the caretakers have always generously received my brief stopovers on their land for a quick snack or lunch. Be sure to land your kayak at the end of the beach, well away from any of their vacationer's leisure activities, and stop into the main house to ask permission to linger if you are planning on having an extended lunch.

Once you leave Camp Merryelande, the flat point of the island ends and you begin heading up the southwestern/Potomac side of the island. The water remains as shallow here as it was on the inner side of the island, with the depth not reaching deeper than 6 feet until you are almost 1 mile offshore. Thus, you can paddle quite peacefully a good distance from shore and still be far removed from any of the powerboat traffic of the open Potomac. Pine trees dominate the landscape with scattered new and older homes nestled amongst their shady grandeur. In the last mile the island narrows, and a riprap seawall protects the land here, because any further erosion would drown the tip of the island entirely. Lying offshore of the island you will see a couple of pound nets, similar to other nets that are scattered in the water around the island, and around the Chesapeake Bay. This fish trap is composed of a long net that is set perpendicular from the shore and the normal migration routes of fish. When fish reach an obstruction they almost invariably head for deeper water, and upon reaching the outer portion of the net they are funneled into the heart-shaped "pound." The fish can enter easily enough but cannot navigate their way back out. The waterman comes periodically to check the net and to empty out his catch for transport to market.

As you approach the bridge, you may notice large tankers docked at a point that is about 1 mile to the northwest of the island. These are fuel tankers unloading their cargo at the fuel docks on Piney Point, and are an impressively large sight. Use caution when rounding the tip of the island and paddling under the bridge. Depending on the stage of the tide, the current can flow strongly through this narrow channel. There are often fishermen lining the shoreline here, occasionally fishing from the bridge, so beware of getting tangled in their lines. Once through the bridge you are back at the landing. You can continue to poke up St. George's Creek or cross over to the heavily forested opposite shoreline and explore Price Cove. I prefer to stop where I started, because there is something noble in a pure circumnavigation, although really all you are doing is messing around in boats.

2. McIntosh Run

> **Length:** The distance from the upstream landing to mouth of the
>   McIntosh and back is about 7 to 9 miles, depending on the
>   amount of general meandering that is done.
> **Put-in Site:** A specific kayak dock located next to MD 5 by the

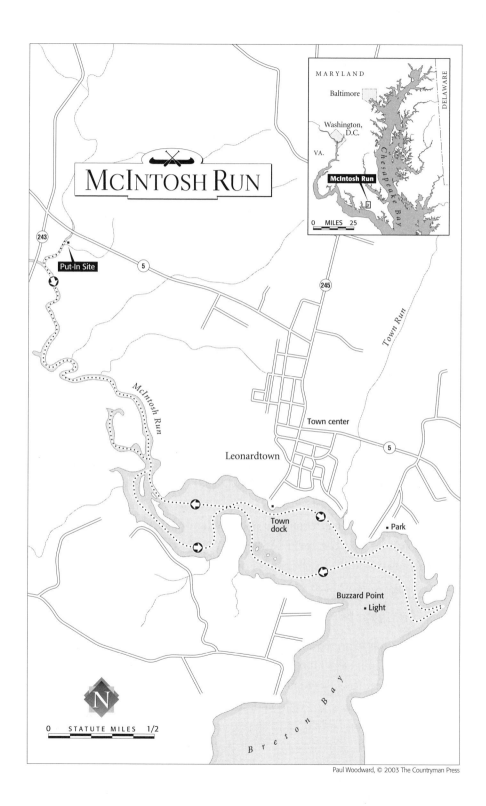

McIntosh Run

Put-In Site

MARYLAND
Baltimore
Washington, D.C.
VA.
McIntosh Run
Chesapeake Bay
DELAWARE
0 MILES 25

McIntosh Run

Town Run

Town center

Leonardtown

Town dock

Park

Buzzard Point
Light

N

0 STATUTE MILES 1/2

Breton Bay

Paul Woodward, © 2003 The Countryman Press

bridge that spans the creek. There are plans for a boat livery here in the future. Public parking is in the large lot next to the launch site. There is no fee; the contact number for information is 301-475-9791.

Driving Directions: MD 5 is accessible from exit 7A on I-495 or from US 301, which joins with MD 5 for a few miles in Waldorf before MD 5 branches off to the south. Follow MD 5 for about 31 miles from US 301. Take a right on MD 243 at a traffic light. Take the second left onto an unmarked road, just before a small bridge and follow this back to the landing, which is by two warehouse buildings.

MCINTOSH RUN creases the agrarian landscape of St. Mary's County, flowing through tobacco fields and Amish pastureland before emptying into the headwaters of Breton Bay along the shoreline of historic Leonardtown. While I love paddling the lush green waterways of Maryland that are preserved by our state parks, there is something wonderful about paddling anonymous waterways like the McIntosh. Kayaking these creeks is not unlike hiking in England and Ireland where the laws of right-of-way allow any trekker to pass over private land. The holistic approach to outdoor recreation, which views farms and wilderness more similar than not, is refreshing. There is a feeling of partnership and understanding between this freshwater river and the surrounding community. Its banks are clean and well tended by the area's residents. This community has installed a dock so that kayakers can enjoy the waterway, not just the local residents. We should all thank them for reaching out to the kayaking community.

Paddling Notes

The launch is a wooden walkway that leads to a low, kayak length, wooden dock. Depending on the day's water depth, you may be able to head under the bridge to poke around upstream. However, the majority of your paddle is to the right and downstream. Note the strength of the flow before you launch. During periods of high rain the current may become too strong for a return trip, even overpowering the tide, in which case you can leave a shuttle at the public park on Camp Calvert Road at the mouth of the McIntosh.

The creek parallels MD 243 for the first ¼ mile and then turns a hard left to the southeast and away from any noise of civilization. During this section, the waterway is little more than a stream, running shallow and narrow through a wooded pastoral landscape of hardwood and holly trees. This mature riparian (riverside) forest and the rolling farm fields behind it form a vivid display of color and light in every season. In spring both the fields and trees sprout bright emerald green; in summer the fields mature and turn a greenish gold and the foliage casts a cool, dappled shade on the water. The most dramatic display comes in autumn when the fields are golden and the trees are dripping with a rainbow of color. A paddle on McIntosh Run, while shorter than most Chesapeake journeys, places the kayaker in Maryland's agrarian heartland like no other trip on the western shore.

Narrow streams begin to empty into the McIntosh, with the run slowly widening and deepening for the rest of your journey. The vege-

Andrea Nolan

Kayak dock on McIntosh Run

tation gradually changes into freshwater marsh and pine trees and about 1 mile from the boat landing you will pass a large red cedar and a persimmon tree on the left at the edge of a small clearing. The persimmon produces yellow flowers in the spring but is most recognizable in the summer and fall as its large orange berries develop. When they ripen in autumn the persimmon berries are delicious, tasting similar to sweet dates; however, before the berry is tender and mature the fruit is vile and full of tannin. Native American communities dried the fruit for the winter and also made bread with its pulp. More recently, the hardwood was also valued as a source for golf club heads. This is an excellent spot for a slice of solitude. As always, respect the fact that this farm is private property and leave the area cleaner than when you arrived.

The run continues to widen and deepen until it spills into the open water delta of the McIntosh's mouth. You will come to the first of several islands in the run's outflow, all of which are navigable on either side. If you paddle to right of the first island you can then take another hard right to explore a gut that cuts back northward paralleling the river. It is a fun little detour and allows another opportunity to experience the delta of the McIntosh, which is unassumingly beautiful as it curls into the open tidal plain. The shores remain wooded with an expansive buffer of freshwater marsh. Large rafts of waterfowl can be found in the wide basin during the spring and fall migration seasons. Past the islands, to the left (east) you will see the multitude of pilings at Leonardtown's old town dock at the end of Washington Street. While the dock is closed for launching boats, you should be able to find a spot to land your kayak for the ¼-mile stroll up into the charming little town. Leonardtown has been the town seat of St. Mary's County since the middle of the 17th century and I recommend forgoing the brown bag lunch for lunch at one of the local restaurants. While this is hardly a high crime area, it is always a good idea to bring a cable to lock your boat up when leaving it for any length of time—it would be bad to be stuck down the creek without a boat.

After the town dock, continue your paddle another ½ mile to where the McIntosh ends at the headwaters of Breton Bay. Buzzard

Point is to your right (south) with some houses on its point. To the left is a shallow cove with a tiny little public park and kayak landing. Straight across is a large farm with one of the best waterfront locations on the bay. The narrow entrance to Glebe Run is on the far end of the idyllic cove and depending on the tide you may be able to explore this little run. The rest of Breton Bay is wide, somewhat trafficked by power-boats and generally more developed along the shoreline, so I do not find any need to paddle further downstream when the quiet solitude of the McIntosh is waiting upstream. Even the most die-hard distance hounds will be lulled into the slower pastoral pace of the McIntosh and the allure of wasting away a wonderful day poking along its quiet banks and drifting on its shaded waters.

3.   *Allen's Fresh Run/Zekiah Swamp*

Length: This trip is a comfortable 8 to 10 miles. There is room for an ambitious extension for strong paddlers into Newport Run, which could lengthen your trip to a total of 12 to 20 miles. I have not included a description of this area, but it can be navigated with the use of a map.

Put-in Site: This is an unofficial kayak landing at the end of an unimproved state dirt road. There is limited parking at the end of the road, so it is best to carpool if paddling with a group and park any cars not bearing boats up on the main road. There are no rest rooms or other facilities at this landing; your only company here will be occasional fishermen.

Driving Directions: Four miles north of the Potomac River, turn onto MD 234/Budd's Creek Road (take a left if traveling south-bound from Maryland, or a right if traveling northbound from Virginia). Follow MD 234 for about 1 mile. Immediately after crossing a bridge over Allen's Fresh Run/Zekiah Swamp you should look for a dirt road on your left. It is about 100 feet past the first bridge and before the second bridge. The dirt road is unmarked, so drive slowly or you will miss it. It is a badly potholed paved road, with trees hugging both sides. The road ends at the water.

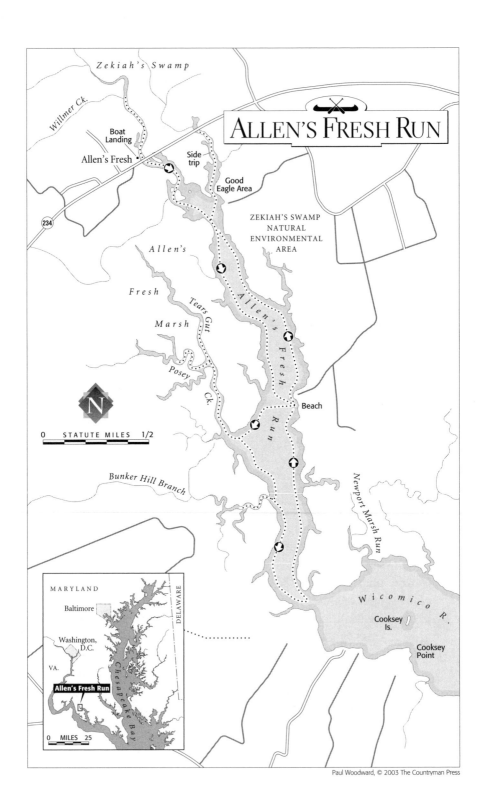

ALLEN'S FRESH RUN

Zekiah's Swamp

Willmer Ck.

Boat
Landing

Allen's Fresh

Side
trip

Good
Eagle Area

234

ZEKIAH'S SWAMP
NATURAL
ENVIRONMENTAL
AREA

Allen's

Fresh

Tears Gut

Marsh

Posey Ck.

Allen's Fresh Run

N

0   STATUTE MILES   1/2

Beach

Bunker Hill Branch

Newport Marsh Run

MARYLAND

Baltimore

Washington,
D.C.

VA.

Allen's Fresh Run

DELAWARE

Chesapeake Bay

Wicomico R.

Cooksey
Is.

Cooksey
Point

0   MILES   25

Paul Woodward, © 2003 The Countryman Press

IDEALLY a kayak trip is like a good novel, grabbing your attention in the beginning, settling into a good rhythm for the bulk of the text and then wowing you in the end. Places that offer both great beginnings and endings can be tough to find, but Allen's Fresh Run is one such location. The beginning, downstream portion takes you through an area with one of the most visible and active populations of bald eagle in Maryland. The end of day explorations wind through the upstream sections of the Zekiah Swamp—a magical forested labyrinth where woods and water merge. In between the start and the end is a paddle for both poke-boaters and distance paddlers, with the wide waters of Allen's Fresh Run punctuated with small guts and creeks ripe for exploring in an area where I have yet to see another boater on the water.

Paddling Notes

Paddle left from the landing to head downriver, and after passing under the bridge for MD 234 you will come upon a wide patch of water with lush sweeping marshland framed by forest and a couple of farms. The marsh pops up throughout the run's waterway, forming numerous small islands to pick your way around. By heading this direction first, you have an excellent chance of spotting the numerous bald eagles that are best seen in this area in the morning hours before the noonday sun drives the fish (and the eagle's prey) into the cooler depths. While you may spot the large birds at all sections of your journey, they seem to be most highly concentrated in this area by the bridge. On one trip I spotted five eagles, including two juveniles devouring a large rockfish on one of the larger marsh islands. Plan on lingering in this eagle haven for a while, and check your watch before moving on to allow yourself one hour at the end of your day to paddle upstream into Zekiah Swamp.

The waterway is broad and the lack of other boat traffic creates a serene paddle where the kayaker is king. About 2 miles below the bridge you will come upon a sandy beach with a pier and some farmland backing up to it. This is one of the few dry land spots in the area. If you stop here, represent the kayaking community well and respect the

Andrea Nolan

Allen's Fresh Run, framed by forest and farmland

farmer's property rights; leave no trace, and stay below mean high-tide line because the intertidal area is public domain.

Across the water from the beach is the entrance to Posey Creek, which I recommend exploring. Tall marsh grasses tightly border the creek, enveloping and transporting you to a different world. After about ½ mile the creek forks, with Tears Gut continuing on north and Posey Creek forking off left to the west. Muskrat call these guts home and you will likely spot one of their homes made out of a mound of grass and mud. Plenty of turtle, waterfowl and heron activity can also be found. You can poke around for approximately a mile in this winding little creek.

Continuing south on the main run, several small guts flow through the marsh south of Posey, and while all are smaller, they are well worth exploring. In about 1½ miles of poking and paddling you will reach the mouth of Allen's Fresh Run and the beginning of the Wicomico River. I usually turn around here in order to allow ample time for exploring Zekiah's Swamp. However, for those with the desire for more distance, you can explore Allen's Fresh Run's neighboring twin, Newport Run.

Bald Eagles

Witnessing people seeing a bald eagle for the first time is one of guiding's absolute joys. The reaction is always the same mixture of awe and reverence, and I have enjoyed watching my clients in this moment even more than watching the eagles soar. This response is heightened by the fact that the eagles were near extinction only 30 ago, primarily due to inadvertent poisoning by the pesticide DDT. DDT weakened the shell of the eagle's eggs and so generations of birds were wiped out. Since DDT was banned in 1972 the bay's eagle population has slowly recovered, growing from a population of 41 nesting pairs in 1977 to a population of 270 nesting pairs in 2000 with another 500 immature, non-nesting eagles also counted. Spotting eagles is no longer a rarity and I have seen hundreds in the bay area, but the reverence and amazement never dissipates.

With its dark brown body, white head, and white tail the mature bald eagle can be easily identified. Its wingspan is broad, reaching up to 8 feet, and the flight of the eagle is characterized by a flat and steady soaring easily distinguished from the rocking dihedral (wings bent upwards in a "V") of vultures, even when spotted from a great distance. This graceful flight and impressive size also helps when identifying immature eagles, which are less distinctive with a uniform brown body and head that becomes mottled with age until the head and tail fully emerge during their fifth year.

The bald eagle is not a picky eater and acts both as a predator and a scavenger. Its preferred food is fish, both dead and alive, but it will also kill birds and small mammals and will eat whatever carrion and tasty human garbage it can find. It is the largest raptor on the bay, so it also throws it weight around and bullies vultures and osprey out of their food. From spring to autumn the eagles are generally solitary or are in breeding pairs if mature. In particularly good feeding areas, like Zekiah's Swamp, there can be a loose colony of nests. The nests are about 8 feet across and 12 feet deep and are usually built below the tree canopy in the main fork of an evergreen tree. To spot an eagle, scan the upper middle tree line for the distinctive white head and look skyward for its flat winged soaring. We have spotted eagles at every location listed in this book, so if you paddle enough, you will see our majestic national bird.

Unlike the 1,500 miles that Alaskan bald eagles fly in their annual migration, the bald eagles of the Chesapeake are year round residents. Our eagles' migration from their summer nests to their winter roosts is a matter of a mere 20 or 30 miles. The winter months are the social season, with groups numbering 100 or more all gathering around the same feeding ground. In 2001, 99 eagles were counted at Blackwater Wildlife Refuge, 188 at Aberdeen Proving Grounds (between the Gunpowder River and the Susquehanna Flats) and 51 around the Conowingo Dam on the Susquehanna River. Eagles in these numbers is an astonishing sight and all the more reason for kayakers to invest in a dry suit, develop their skills and extend their paddling season. —*A.N.*

Andrea Nolan

Prime eagle habitat on Allen's Fresh Run

Paddle to the left and about ½ mile straight east of the mouth you will pass little Cooksey Island and another ½ mile past that you will reach the entrance to Newport Run. There is a delta island that has been deposited at the mouth of the run, and you can paddle up either side of the island to enter the Newport. From here on up my description ends and your exploration begins. Enjoy.

On your return trip up Allen's Fresh Run I recommend taking a short side trip up Old Mill Branch which branches off to the right just prior to the bridge. Its narrow passage wanders though an area that seems like a meticulously landscaped water garden with miniature islands, delicate flowers, and painted turtles sunning themselves on logs.

In your final hour on the water, kayak past the landing and into Zekiah Swamp. Depending on the water levels, you should be able to travel 1 to 2 miles into the swamp. The waterway bends to and fro amongst trees that soar up from the banks, enclosing you within a tunnel of greenery. Farther upstream the forest and river become one as the trees depart the shoreline for the water, creating the labyrinth of the freshwater swamp. The Zekiah is a headwater and border swamp, where the distinction between the forest and the waterline becomes blurred, with trees growing both in and outside of the water. Common swamp trees include red maple and green ash, and many shrubs such as jewelweed, milkweed and common alder are also found under the trees' canopy. The diversity of the swamp is even greater than the marsh, and you would do well to bring a good plant guide to your exploration of this waterway. Beware that poison ivy also thrives in this wet environment. Beaver dams and fallen trees will occasionally block your way, but it is worth dragging your kayak over a log or two. The impediments will either become too much, or eventually the water flow will be too fast or shallow and you will have to turn back. But until you reach that point, paddle ever onward because you are a kayaker in the Chesapeake and Zekiah Swamp is where a kayaker is meant to be.

4. *Mattawoman Creek*

Length: The total trip length is 8 miles, with much more mileage available by extending your trip further downstream.

Put-in Site: Mattingly Landing. There is a port-a-john at the landing. The $5 fee is on the envelope honor system—fee is for trailers only, but we recommend paying for launching your kayak since the money is for maintaining the landing. The park is open from sunrise to sunset.

Driving Directions: From I-495 East/DC Beltway, exit onto MD 210 South/Indianhead Highway. Follow until the end of the road, which is in the town of Indian Head (about 30 minutes from 495). Just before the Naval Base take a left onto Mattingly Avenue. Follow to the end of the road and park at the boat landing.

MATTAWOMAN CREEK is an unassuming tributary of the Potomac River, less than 1 hour from the Washington Monument. It is bordered by the Indian Head Naval Station, and is across the Potomac River from the Quantico Marine Corps Base and the FBI training headquarters. Despite these imposing neighbors, after only a few paddle strokes on the Mattawoman, a kayaker is transported to a serene natural world. While not as glamorous as the Pocomoke River or as pristine as Blackwater

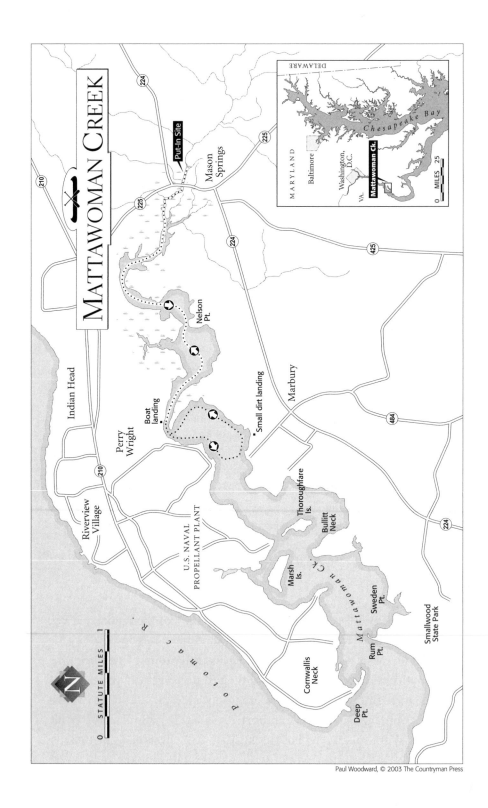

MATTAWOMAN CREEK

Put-In Site

Mason Springs

Nelson Pt.

Small dirt landing

Marbury

Boat landing

Perry Wright

Indian Head

Riverview Village

U.S. NAVAL PROPELLANT PLANT

Thoroughfare Is.

Bullitt Neck

Marsh Is.

Sweden Pt.

Cornwallis Neck

Deep Pt.

Rum Pt.

Smallwood State Park

Mattawoman Ck.

Potomac R.

210

224

225

224

425

484

224

N

0   STATUTE MILES   1

DELAWARE

MARYLAND

Baltimore

Washington, D.C.

VA.

Mattawoman Ck.

Chesapeake Bay

0   MILES   25

Paul Woodward, © 2003 The Countryman Press

Wildlife Refuge, this creek is the utility player of my paddling lineup with its easy access from Washington, D.C., and beautiful woods and marshlands. On my maiden voyage here in the autumn of 1998, Mike and I watched an eight-point buck swim across the creek. We spotted him in the shadows of the northern bank, and after we paused the buck calmly entered the water. He swam with strong surges through the creek, as confident as a Labrador retriever in the water. Upon reaching the other side he gracefully exited the water and slipped into the shadows of the woods. A few miles up the Potomac, Washington, D.C., was bustling with importance and policy, but on the Mattawoman, that buck was the most powerful thing around.

Paddling Notes

Swing left to head upriver. There is some boat traffic at this point in the river, so it is best to hang to one side or another. Healthy freshwater marshes line the creek here, with spatterdock filling in the width of the creek considerably in the summer. About 1 mile upstream there is a nice gut to explore on the left (north), which cuts through the marsh, terminating at the forested riverbanks. A little farther on is a small sand island, which is also on the left side of the creek. Often there is a power-boat or two beached for a picnic, but there is always room to share. With a hard sand bottom this is a great spot for swimming and also makes for an excellent lunch spot on the way back downstream. Across the river from the island is a several-acre expanse of spatterdock and wetlands backed by a lush forest.

Paddling further upstream you will pass a rope swing with a small grass landing on the left which leads up to the inactive railroad tracks that parallel the water. The creek then makes a wide looping bend to the right, with an old steel retaining wall for the railroad shaping the left shore. From the boat landing to this point you may have been joined by an occasional slow moving recreational fishing boat. As you continue upstream from this point the bends become tighter, the creek narrows, and the downstream flow of the water begins to overpower the tide. This upstream area is purely the domain of human-powered vessels.

With the appearance of gravel bottoms the wetlands drop away and are replaced by forest. Depending on the tide, kayakers should be able to make it past the bridge for MD 225 before your boats scrape to a stop in shallow water. When returning back downstream, make sure to take the time to explore some of the side coves and guts. The fallen logs covered with turtles, the red fox stalking the marsh grass, the doe and fawn

Freshwater Marsh Plants

To a person passing on a fast boat or car the marsh looks like a flat, unremarkable sea of green. However, the kayaker travels at plant level and nature's speed, and thus can experience the colorful diversity of the freshwater marsh. Unlike the saltwater or brackish water marshes, the vegetation of the freshwater wetland does not need to adapt to a saltwater environment. Therefore, a small section of wetland can be filled with dozens of species of plants. This diversity supports a variety of animals. Wetlands are important nesting and feeding areas for birds and mammals and they serve as nurseries for young fish and amphibians. The wetland also acts as an effective buffer between land and water, absorbing sediment, nutrient and toxin runoff from the land, and protecting the shoreline from further erosion from boat wakes or storm waves. Each plant fills a certain niche dictated primarily by elevation, with a change of 1 foot providing for entirely different microcosms of life. With all the subtlety of the marsh, it is still fairly easy to view the marsh as three primary vegetation levels: floating aquatic vegetation, emergent vegetation, and marsh.

Floating aquatic vegetation are rooted in riverbed, and are at least partially submerged at all times. They create the elusive boundary between water and marsh, and according to the tide and the season can seem to shrink or expand the river by up to 100 yards or more. The bay's primary species in this niche is the yellow pond lily, named after the single yellow flower that grows in the midst of a flat, waxy green leaf pad that is about 1 foot in diameter. The leaf is supported by a half dollar sized spongy stem that leads beneath the usually thick mud into a massive rhizome root that ties entire fields of lilies into one massive organism and helps buffer the rest of the marshland from waves. Depending on the tide level, the plants will be in 6 inches to 3 feet of water. At high tide the lily pads appear to be free floating on the water, and during the highest water they can become completely submerged. This trait earns the lilies the common name of spatterdock, because after reemerging from its dunking the lily's shiny pad tends to be spattered with sediment deposits.

Emergent vegetation is the next level up, with the plants being partially watching from the forest. This is where the true beauty of the Matta-woman lies and is only visible to the calm and patient paddler. The side guts also afford a beautiful view of the surrounding freshwater marsh vegetation. In some of the narrower guts you may have to back paddle your way out, or attempt a 35-point turn. Just don't end up like some clients of mine who wedged their kayak completely perpendicular to

submerged at high tide and fully exposed at low tide—this is the true boundary between marsh and water. Within the category of emergent vegetation there are three plants that you can expect to see on any fresh-water river: the pickerelweed, arrow arum, and the arrowhead plants. These plants can all look similar and can be easily confused at first. The pickerelweed has dark green heart shaped leaves, with vibrant blue clus-ters of flowers in the summer months. Arrow arum has large arrow shaped leaves that grow up to 3 feet long, and have clusters of white flowers during the summer. Arrowhead looks similar in shape to arrow arum, except for its veins, which distinctly radiate from the stalk unlike the arrow arum's mid-vein. The leaf is smaller, measuring only 1 foot in length, and is often a paler green. Along with acting as an additional buffer against wave action, many of the emergent vegetation's leaves, seeds and roots serve as food for migratory waterfowl.

As the marsh rises out of the constantly submerged muck, the landscape becomes a riot of vegetation, with the dominant species being cattails, wild rice, big cordgrass, and phragmites. Cattails are easily recog-nizable by their distinctive hot dog shaped female flower, topped by the spike of the male flower. Wild rice can grow in large expanses of marsh and are an important food source for birds, particularly for rails and red-winged blackbirds. The rice plant stands about 5 feet high with a foot long feather of small leaves and rice seeds at the top of the grass. Big cordgrass is a native grass that can reach heights of 10 feet, with small sharp flat leaves radiating out from the main stem near the top of the plant. Similar to cordgrass is *Phragmities australis,* an invasive species with little nutritional value for our native bird and animal life. Phrag, as it is commonly known, can grow to about 12 feet tall and is a reed, with leaves growing out from its round stem. The top 1-foot of the plant is a bushy flower head that is the same yellowish color as the rest of the plant. Beyond the grasses, are the numerous moisture hungry shrubs and trees such as marsh mallow, marsh hibiscus, jewelweed and river birch that prefer the riparian (riverside) environment of the Chesapeake and its tributaries. *—A.N.*

View upstream on Mattawoman Creek

the marsh, creating a dam that a beaver would be proud of.

Upon reaching the boat landing you can continue your journey by heading downstream toward open water. You will be leaving the solitude of upstream paddling behind and sharing space with powerboats, so stay close to the edges. In about 1 mile of paddling downstream the creek widens out to a broad mouth, with a line of pilings running the length. On the other side of these pilings speedboats and jet skis can be seen crisscrossing the wide mouth of the river. The right side of the river is occupied by the U.S. Naval Propellant Plant and is a restricted area. Rather than making yourself and the sailors in the base nervous, I recommend crossing to the other side of the creek for the remainder of your paddle. Stay on the upriver side of the pilings while making the crossing and you will stand a greater chance of not getting in the way of those in pursuit of speed. An expansive freshwater marsh will be to your left and the forested shoreline of Smallwood State Park will be in front of you. Once across you will be in the general vicinity of a small dirt landing that is popular amongst local nocturnal revelers. Despite the beer cans, this is the area where I have often spotted bald eagles; one once swept down from a tree to glide just feet above my head. If you swing right you can continue to paddle west toward the mouth of the river and will reach the landings and campgrounds of Smallwood State Park in about 2 miles. If launching or landing from the park, move fast, because the ramps are heavily trafficked by boat trailers. The creek joins with the Potomac River in another 3 miles. While the river is pretty here, with some interesting islands to explore, the boat traffic is heavy on weekends. My preferred trip once crossing the creek is to backtrack to Mattingly by wandering amongst the marsh—it is the perfect size to lose yourself in without being in danger of getting truly lost. The area is much too shallow for even the most foolhardy jet skier, so your only companions will be muskrat and red-winged blackbirds. You may occasionally have to backtrack or scoot across some mud, but you can never make a wrong turn in such a glorious area, and getting lost is a great excuse for lingering in beauty.

5. *Parker Creek*

> **Length:** The open water paddle to reach Parker Creek is 5 miles, one way. You can usually paddle about 2 miles upstream on the creek, thus the total trip mileage is about 14 miles.
>
> **Put-in Site:** The launch site is Breezy Point Marina (410-535-9020). There are two boat landings at the far end of the small marina's row of boat slips. The strip of grass to the side of the landings can be used for staging your trip without blocking the ramps. The marina's owner has been considering putting in a landing just for kayakers, and likely will do that if use of his fa-

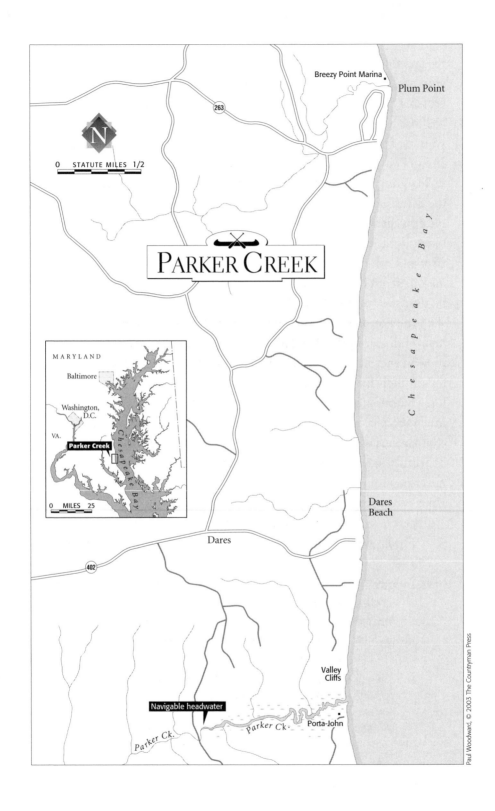

Breezy Point Marina

Plum Point

263

Chesapeake Bay

N

0   STATUTE MILES   1/2

PARKER CREEK

MARYLAND

Baltimore

Washington, D.C.

VA.

Parker Creek

Chesapeake Bay

0   MILES   25

Dares Beach

Dares

402

Valley Cliffs

Navigable headwater

Parker Ck.

Parker Ck.

Porta-John

cility increases. Currently the daily rate for use of the landing is $8; the seasonal rate is $85. There are bathroom facilities.

Driving Directions: MD 4 is accessible from US 301 and I-495. Follow MD 4/Pennsylvania Avenue East until you take a left onto MD 260 East 6 miles after you pass US 301. Continue all the way until it ends at the Bay in Chesapeake Beach and then take a right onto MD 261. Follow this through the town of Chesapeake Beach and continue on 261 for about 5 miles. Turn left on Breezy Point Road (there should be a road sign for Breezy Point or Breezy Point Campgrounds). Follow all the way to the bay where you will see a gated entrance to Breezy Point Campgrounds on your left and the Breezy Point Marina on your right. Follow the road into the Breezy Point Marina. Bear to the right, around the boat slips. The boat landings are on the far end of the parking lot.

OVER THE MILLENNIA, Parker Creek has carved a flat river valley in the midst of the steep sand shores of the Calvert Cliffs formation that stretches from Chesapeake Beach to the mouth of the Patuxent. This hollow in the midst of cliffs, with the eastern shore a distant smudge on the horizon, is a wilderness destination that beckons to any experienced paddler ready for the open water journey. Parker Creek's watershed is protected by a union of the Nature Conservancy, the Maryland Department of Natural Resources, and private landowners, with the stewardship of the land capably managed by the American Chestnut Land Trust and its on-site caretakers. This conservation effort has kept the beach wild and both sides of the creek flourishing and green. The journey to reach Parker is a destination unto itself, involving a paddle over 5 miles on the bay as you pass cliffs to the west and expansive blue water to the east. Like all open water excursions, qualified kayakers who have monitored the day's weather forecast should be the only paddlers to undertake this trip. The fetch across such a wide distance can create some large swells and breaking surf, and the high cliffs allow little protection from sudden storms.

Near the navigable headwater of Parker Creek

Paddling Notes

Breezy Point Marina is located on Plum Point Creek. From the landing, head to the right for a couple strokes and then to the left to leave the creek, paddling along the water's edge to stay clear of boat traffic. Swing your bow to the right to head south when you leave Plum Point Creek. The next 5 miles of your paddle will be along a scenic sand cliff shoreline. The water depth remains shallow for a couple hundred yards from the shore, but even beyond that point it is rare to have other boaters near your paddling course, since they are en route elsewhere. These conditions make the next 5 miles a liberating experience of paddling in a boundary-free environment without the worries of being run over, running aground, or negotiating tight meanders. The cliffs are your constant companions with an occasional lowering of altitude and some groupings of houses. The largest community that you will pass is Dare's Beach, 4 miles south of Breezy Point. There are several small beaches between Dares Beach and the entrance to Parker Creek, and they are all fertile picking grounds for fossilized shark's teeth (described in the Chesapeake Beach description.)

The land between Dare's Beach and Parker is protected as wilderness. You cannot miss the entrance to Parker—it is an unmistakable broad river valley in the midst of cliffs. There is a sandy beach to the north of the mouth, and a larger beach expanse to the south. The shores of Parker Creek are composed primarily of thick mud, so you should use the beach for any rest or lunch breaks. While on the beach you need to tread lightly. The primary reason this land has been singled out for protection is that the beach is one of the last places in the world that the endangered tiger beetle is found. Since the tiger beetle lives in the sands above the high-tide line, all foot traffic should be restricted to below the mean high tide (distinguishable by the line of flotsam that is deposited at the highest reaches of the tide). Near the southern end of the south beach is a pathway that leads to a grassy clearing. The mosquitoes here are ferocious, but for the thick skinned there is a port-a-john at the other side of the small clearing.

The entrance to Parker is a shallow delta with a wandering channel of deeper water. During an ebbing tide the current can be extremely

Broad downstream section of Parker Creek

Mike Savario

Tides

The Chesapeake is a gentle place, and generally speaking so are its tides, with a usual range of 1 to 3 feet. However, although our tides are small, they do exist and do fluctuate, so it is good to be familiar with their movement before venturing into the bay. The Chesapeake has four tides a day, two high and two low, with each flow lasting for six hours and then separated by a ½-hour long slack tide. Since it takes 26 hours to complete a tide cycle, the time of the high and low tides changes daily. Most marinas carry charts of their local tides, along with tide guides for the entire bay which may require you to add or subtract hours based on your position relative to the central position used by the tide chart. You can also use various weather Internet sites for current and projected tides.

Since the tides are caused by the gravitational pull of the moon, the tidal range increases when the sun and moon are in line during the new moon and the full moon. These periods are termed spring tides and their reach can be several feet above normal. Neap tides are weak tides that occur in the time when the moon and sun are at right angles, with the pull so diminished that the tide can sometimes be hardly evident. Tides are not restricted to the bay proper, but spill into all of its tributaries, at first mixing with the river water creating a brackish environment, and in its last few miles simply pushing the fresh water back and forth creating an area of tidal fresh water. Generally speaking, the currents that accompany even our spring tides are not strong, so you do not need to plan

strong, occasionally too strong to paddle against. If this is the case, you can launch your kayak on the inside of the delta, from the southern beach. The water drops off precipitously here, and the current can still be strong, so be ready to paddle hard for your first 20 feet, until you make it out of the tidal current.

Parker Creek is a powerful example of how in nature, a straight line is not the most efficient way between two points. The creek meanders almost a dozen times in the course of 2 miles, with each meander leading you deeper and deeper into beauty. The environment at the mouth of the creek is brackish, however as you head further upstream it changes into a tidal freshwater environment, with more diverse vegetation. The river valley also begins to narrow. What began as a flat valley, becomes increasingly compressed between the encroaching forested banks. While the river valley narrows, the wide meanders of the creek your trip solely around the tide chart. However, all of the bay's tidal currents can be magnified by heavy rains or by wind.

Tidal currents also increase whenever water is compressed rapidly from a wide to narrow passageway, such as between bridge pilings, narrow harbors and channels. The effect of these restricted areas is similar to putting your thumb over a hose nozzle. The key is to be alert. You usually can paddle against the current in these areas, but be especially aware of breaching if you are paddling with the current, particularly under bridges.

While you usually do not need to plan around the bay's tides, it is still a good idea to monitor the current and paddle with the flow whenever possible. Using the tidal current for even a portion of your trip can dramatically ease fatigue and lengthen the distance you can cover. Besides planning around currents, you also need to monitor the ebb (retreating) and flood (rising) tides, because the topography of the bay is such that it can take 1/4 mile for the elevation to change 1 foot. Thus, while you were able to travel to the head of a gut at midtide, if you wait to return downstream at low tide you may be forced to slog through thick, exposed mud. Likewise, if you fail to pull your kayak well up onto a gently sloping beach or marsh, you may have the experience of watching your kayak float away upstream while you are eating your lunch. I speak from experience, having learned both of these lessons the hard way.
—A.N.

begin to touch the forest edges at the top of each bend. It is not uncommon to spot deer in the forest and fields along the edges of the marsh. Eagle and osprey both nest in this area, and there are active muskrat and beaver populations as well. Be careful when paddling the curves of the meanders; the inside corners are where sediment is deposited. You can become easily grounded, with just flopping mummichogs for company.

A trail comes down to the top (northern) bend of the last of the major meanders. At high tide it is possible to get out onto this trail without too much difficulty. However, you will sink deep within the river mud if you attempt wading ashore at low tide. After this trail, the river steadily narrows and the wide meanders cease. What you lose of the scenic vistas of the downriver marshland is replaced by the mystery of winding tunnels of trees. A beaver dam in the uppermost stretches of the water will ultimately stop your progress. Here spatterdock and cattails prevail as the vegetation of choice, and the water is crystal clear due to the filtering qualities of the dam.

When you paddle back downstream, remember to be ready for a possible strong current in the mouth of the creek. If the tide is ebbing and the wind is blowing westward across the bay there can be small breaking waves to punch through. The habitat south of the creek is much like that to the north, with the community of Scientist's Cliffs lining the shoreline about 1 mile south of the Parker. When I am within Parker Creek, and on the wild beaches surrounding that waterway, I can forget that I am not alone on the bay. The 5 miles back to Breezy Point are just enough to ease me out of my blissful wilderness stupor and back into the real world.

6. *Chesapeake Beach*

Length: The total trip length is about 18 miles. You shorten the route to 10 miles by omitting the journey into Fishing Creek. You could leave a shuttle vehicle Fishing Creek Marina and create a 13-mile trip.

Put-in Site: The launch site is Breezy Point Marina (410-535-9020). There are two boat landings at the far end of the small marina's row of boat slips. The strip of grass to the side of the landings can be used for staging your trip without blocking the ramps. The marina's owner has been considering putting in a landing just for kayakers, and likely will do that if use of his facility increases. Currently the daily rate for use of the landing is $8; the seasonal rate is $85. There are bathroom facilities.

Driving Directions: MD 4 is accessible from US 301 and I-495. Follow MD 4/Pennsylvania Avenue East until you take a left onto Rt. 260 East 6 miles after you pass 301. Continue all the way until it ends at the bay in Chesapeake Beach and then take a right onto MD 261. Follow this through the town of Chesapeake Beach and continue on 261 for about 5 miles. Turn left on Breezy Point Road (there should be a road sign for Breezy Point or Breezy Point Campgrounds). Follow all the way to the bay where you will see a gated entrance to Breezy Point

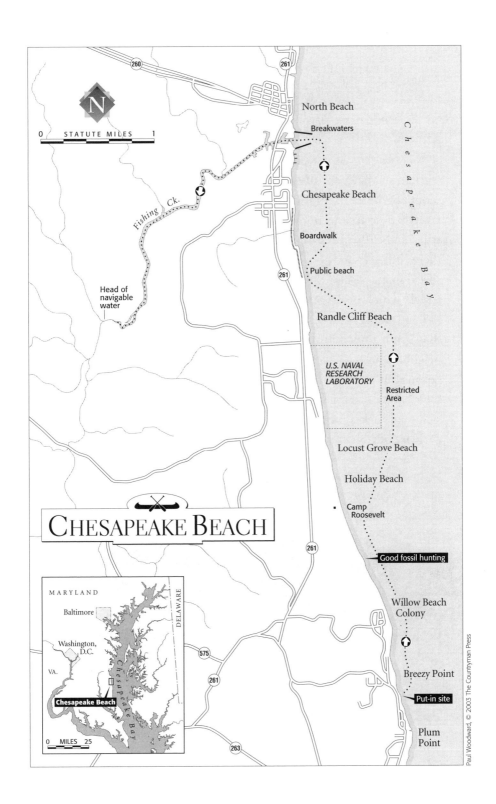

N

0 STATUTE MILES 1

North Beach

Breakwaters

Chesapeake Bay

Fishing Ck.

Chesapeake Beach

Boardwalk

Public beach

Head of
navigable
water

261

Randle Cliff Beach

*U.S. NAVAL
RESEARCH
LABORATORY*

Restricted
Area

Locust Grove Beach

Holiday Beach

261

Camp
Roosevelt

CHESAPEAKE BEACH

Good fossil hunting

Willow Beach
Colony

MARYLAND

Baltimore

Washington,
D.C.

VA.

Chesapeake Bay

Breezy Point

Put-in site

Chesapeake Beach

DELAWARE

575

261

Plum
Point

0 MILES 25

263

Paul Woodward, © 2003 The Countryman Press

Campgrounds on your left and the Breezy Point Marina on your right. Follow the road into the Breezy Point Marina. Bear to the right, around the boat slips. The boat landings are on the far end of the parking lot.

THE CHESAPEAKE BEACH AREA marks the beginning of the Calvert Cliffs formation that continues all the way down to Drum Point, at the mouth of the Patuxent River. Along with Parker Creek, this is one of the few trip descriptions in this book that consists of a primarily open bay trip. Sand cliffs, about 100 feet high, border the bay, and at the base of these cliffs are sandy beaches, rich with fossils—particularly black fossilized shark's teeth from the Miocene epoch. An exploration up Fishing Creek, which bisects the town of Chesapeake Beach, offers visually striking scenery and open bay paddling. It is an anonymous little creek that is not unlike hundreds of similar waterways that run through neighborhoods all over Maryland—full of perch, crabs, and great blue herons but little known or explored by anyone who does not live on their banks. Fishing Creek's quiet, grass-lined meanderings and deep, rich mud makes for a wonderful contrast to the open, salty, sandy experience of Chesapeake Beach.

The quiet waters of Fishing Creek

Andrea Nolan

The cliffs of Chesapeake Beach

Paddling Notes

When you leave the marina and Plum Creek you need to swing your bow to the left to head north up the bay toward Chesapeake Beach. You will pass the long, wide recreation beach of Breezy Point and then sand cliffs will dominate the scenery. The water remains relatively shallow a considerable distance from shore; even 200 hundred yards out the water is rarely deeper than 7 feet over a sandy bottom.

The cliffs are colorful, with the older lower section of bluish clay supporting the younger, upper layers of yellow sand. The sediment that creates Calvert Cliffs was deposited during the Miocene epoch, 10 to 20 million years ago, and the beaches between Breezy Point and Chesapeake Beach are good areas for fossil hunting since they are isolated and not as picked-over as the shores nearer to town. Waves, storms, and gravity are constantly eroding the cliffs, exposing the fossils of marine animals that have been preserved within the sand, and washing them into the bay. Do not dig or climb on the cliffs, as they can and will break apart, creating dangerous landslides. The best place to find fossils is the low-tide line, where the fossils are deposited after being scoured clean by the bay's waters. Whale, dolphin, bird, ray, and mollusk fossils can all be found along the beach, but the most prevalent and popular fossils are shark's teeth. The shark's teeth range in size from 1 millimeter to several inches long and can always be found by the water's edge. They are black and are unmistakably shaped like sharp teeth. About 1½ miles north of Breezy Point the beaches are mostly composed of the slick, bluish clay and are generally not good for landing.

About 2½ miles from Breezy Point you will pass the Naval Research Laboratory. The red and white towers of the lab are prominent and the pier of the lab sticks out rather far into the bay. It is prohibited to get within ½ mile of the shore in this area that runs about ⅔ of a mile long. Good sand beaches exist north of the Naval Station and in about 1 mile

Wind

While the Chesapeake's tides may be gentle, our wind can be a formidable force and needs to be factored into route and trip planning. Air acts like water, and generates wind by flowing from high pressure to low pressure areas, often along a storm front. Wind can also be locally generated, along the same principles. When the sun rapidly heats the land, it radiates warm air, which rises, thus lowering the near ground air pressure, causing strong winds to develop. These local winds generally cease when the land cools at sunset. The extended force of the bay's winds can overpower the normal tidal flow, even completely reversing a neap tide. The winds of a strong northeaster can seem to push all of the water out of the bay, exposing large stretches of river bottom. Conversely, a strong southern wind can hold water in the rivers, creating tides so high that you can paddle down Dock Street in Annapolis. Waves are created by these same winds, with an area transforming from a beginner's paddle to a rough water challenge in the course of a day.

Thus, while it is nice to get a tide chart for an area, you must find out what the water is really doing by checking the wind forecast. These forecasts are available from the weather channel, the Internet (see appendix) or from a portable weather radio, which is available at any marine or electronics store. Predictions can be wrong, and area topography can funnel and change the wind's direction, so you must also learn how to read the wind speed once you reach your paddling site. A helpful guide to this is the Beaufort Wind Scale (see appendix), which provides practical gauges of the wind, with wind speed given in knots (nautical you will come to the public beach of the town of Chesapeake Beach, which is a popular recreation spot on any warm weekend day. The beach can be a destination unto itself, where you may opt for sunning and relaxing over the further exertion of paddling up Fishing Creek. There are port-a-john's here, usually stationed at the beginning of the boardwalk that runs along the shore and ends at the condo development next to the Chesapeake Beach railroad museum. The boardwalk was constructed in the early years of this millennium, but this is not the first time a boardwalk has rimmed the shoreline. Chesapeake Beach was a booming summer resort town from 1900–30 thanks to the Chesapeake Beach railroad, which transported Washington, D.C., residents the 28 miles from the city to the cool breezes of the bay. There were roller coasters, casinos and all sorts of restaurants and hotels built along the boardwalk.

miles per hour, which translates to be the equivalent of 1.15 miles/hour) based on its effect on the water and the trees. Keep in mind that this scale was developed for open water, not small tidal tributaries. The power of the wind to shape waves is determined by the fetch (the distance that a wind moves across), velocity, and the duration of the wind. In an area of great fetch, like the open bay, the wind will generally behave like the Beaufort Scale predicts, with a 20-knot wind creating moderate waves and spray. However, during the same wind, a winding narrow waterway with marsh- or tree-lined edges breaks up the wind's fetch and force, resulting in a reduced power and only small wavelets.

Wind and waves can easily bully around an unprepared sea kayaker. The difference between paddling in 5-knot and 20-knot wind is dramatic. When possible, plan to paddle a route that is in the leeward (sheltered side) of the wind, and when traversing open water paddle parallel with the wind, and perpendicular to the waves, and try to have the wind at your back for the journey home. Waves can also be created by boat wakes, and you must plan on encountering these in any major river or congested area of the bay, such as Annapolis. In narrow rivers with high boat volume, such as the South River, multiple wakes will rebound against one another, and against sea walls *(clapitus)*, creating confused and difficult seas. You must develop your kayaking skills if you wish to paddle in any exposed deeper water/powerboat areas. The effort to improve your abilities pays large dividends, because while kayaking in 25-knot crosswinds will never be leisurely, it can be fun. —A.N.

Waves at Chesapeake Beach during 20-knot wind

After the public beach you can either head back to Breezy Point for a round-trip of 10 miles, or you can continue on into Fishing Creek. For the latter option, head northeast from the beach, veering out into the open water to make it around the breakwater of the harbor. Once you paddle around the breakwater and head in toward Fishing Creek, be alert for incoming and outgoing boats—the Rod and Reel Marina to your left is a popular center for charter boat fishing and the Fishing Creek Marina on the right on the other side of the bridge has nonstop launchings of trailered powerboats on nice weekend days. This marina can serve as a pullout site, where you can drop off a shuttle vehicle by following the driving directions into Chesapeake Beach, but taking a right into the marina before crossing the bridge over Fishing Creek. Past the Fishing Creek Marina the boat traffic disappears and it seems that no one but kayakers have any reason to head upstream. In about ½ mile, after passing a restaurant, some boat slips and a couple of houses, the creek meanders to the right and then back to the left again. From this point on, the creek pretty much exists in its natural state, with just occasional evidence of people or homes. This may change as Chesapeake Beach is experiencing a population and development growth, but hopefully the Critical Area development laws will continue to protect the shoreline. Unlike the open bay, the shorelines here are entirely composed of thick, rich river mud and very few places exist to get out and stretch your legs. After the bends to the left and right you will be on a relatively straight stretch of water followed by a less dramatic bend to the right. From this point on the river generally bends gradually back to the left, toward the south. The upstream portion of the creek is framed by trees and marsh elder and is a delightful place to explore. The contrast of this salty, sleepy creek of mud and green grass, with the open water and high cliffs of the bay is remarkable and serves to heighten the beauty of both areas. It definitely pays to spend the extra miles exploring little Fishing Creek.

7.   *Mattaponi Creek*
and other small tributaries of the Middle Patuxent

Length: Paddling to the top of Mattaponi and back is about 4½ miles. To the top of the Mattaponi and Lyon's Creek the distance is more like 8 miles. To Mattaponi, Lyon's, and Weir the distance grows to 9 miles, and if you include Broad Creek in this lineup you will total about 12 miles. My favorite option is every combination, done repeatedly, in every season, for the rest of my life.

Put-in Site: Patuxent River Park, Selby's Landing. An annual special use permit is required which can be purchased at the park office or by mail for $5 for residents of Prince George's or Montgomery County or $10 for noncounty residents. The phone number for the office is 301-627-6074 and the mailing address is 1600 Croom Airport Road, Upper Marlboro, MD 20772. There is a port-a-john at the landing. The park is open from sunrise to sunset. Maryland–National Capital Park and Planning Commission (M–NCPPC) manages this facility.

Driving Directions: From I-95/495 take Exit 11A, Pennsylvania Avenue S/E (MD 4) and follow for about 8 miles and then exit onto 301 South, for about 2 miles. (An alternate route is to take US 50 to MD 301 South and follow for about 15 miles, to the junction with MD 4, and then use the rest of the directions as written). Take a left on Croom Station Road and follow for 1.6

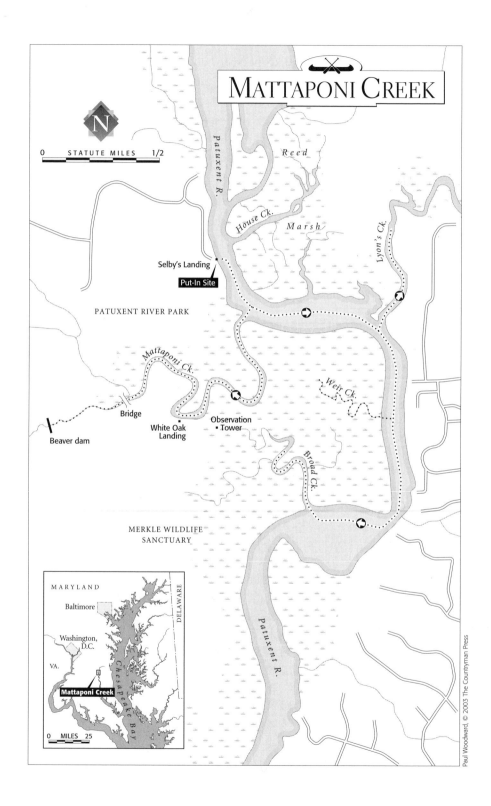

Mattaponi Creek

N

STATUTE MILES

0   1/2

Patuxent R.

Reed

House Ck.

Marsh

Lyon's Ck.

Selby's Landing
Put-In Site

PATUXENT RIVER PARK

Mattaponi Ck.

Weir Ck.

Bridge

White Oak
Landing

Observation
Tower

Broad Ck.

Beaver dam

MERKLE WILDLIFE
SANCTUARY

Patuxent R.

MARYLAND

Baltimore

DELAWARE

Washington,
D.C.

VA.

Mattaponi Creek

Chesapeake Bay

0   MILES   25

Paul Woodward, © 2003 The Countryman Press

miles. Take a left on Croom Road (MD 382 and follow for about
1.5 miles. Take another left on Croom Airport Road (there
should be a Patuxent River Park sign on the right-hand side of
the road). Follow this road until it ends, continuing straight after
the park entrance toward the group camp area (if you need to
buy a permit, you should turn right at the sign for the park office
before continuing on to the landing). At the end of the road,
fork left toward Selby's Landing. The road ends in a small
parking lot and the boat landing is at the bottom of the hill.

IF POSSIBLE, the side tributaries of the Patuxent are more alluring than
the main river itself, but I must admit a bias. My favorite two miles in
the world are the Mattaponi Creek, and I have paddled this stretch
more times than any other place on earth. I have ventured into this
Eden in every season, from times when there was a skim of ice on the
water to days when the water was so warm it was difficult to distinguish
it from the air. I have slid over the still waters reflecting the pink of
dawn, floated along in a raft of canoes containing 30 hollering kids
during crisp October days, and have been lucky enough to lead dozens
of sunset and moonlight paddles along its path. I have had a beaver
swim beside me for several minutes and have rounded a bend to find a
wide-eyed client watching five beavers swim around her kayak under a
bright full moon. The creek is my version of paradise and due to that I
cannot pick a favorite time of day or season for the creek—all time that
I spend on the Mattaponi is perfection. The lushness of the marsh is
unsurpassed by anywhere else that I have traveled. The trip up and back
the Mattaponi is the shortest that we describe in this book, but it is definitely the largest trip in my heart.

Paddling Notes

Selby's Landing is small and used by both powerboaters and paddlers.
Steer clear of clogging up the cement boat ramp by using the gravel/dirt
entry to the right of the ramp. You can unload your gear here without
holding up powerboats from launching on the cement ramp. After

launching, take a right from the landing, making sure to paddle close to the right-hand (western) side due to possible boat traffic. In about 100 yards you will paddle over the wreck of the *Peter Cooper*, which sank July 17, 1887, after catching fire at the mouth of Lyon's Creek where it was supposed to pick up load of topsoil. It either drifted or was towed to its present location. The bow, which points southwest, can be just barely seen under the water at low tide. Continue paddling along the river's right edge and you will come to the entrance to the Mattaponi, about ¼ a mile below Selby's Landing. Depending on the tide and the season, the entrance can appear to be 30 to 1000 yards wide. The wider appearance is deceptive however, because the southern 70 yards of the opening is an expansive bed of spatterdock and is only 1 foot deep at even the highest of tides. At the far southern end of the opening there is an active osprey nest. As soon as you enter the creek you will notice beaver and muskrat activity. As of March 2001 there was a new beaver lodge on the right (northern) side, marking the beginning of the creek, with smaller muskrat houses nearby. Your best chance to see beaver activity is near dawn or dusk. Since the Park is only open to the public during daytime hours, you may want to arrive in the cooler early morning hours to spot beavers. However, even with a midday arrival, if you paddle silently and you are a little lucky you might come upon a beaver at any time. I had a large, fat beaver swim beneath my kayak in the middle of a sunny, hot July day. Keep your eyes alert for a brown head slicing a "v" through the water.

Once in the Mattaponi you can freely paddle in the middle of the creek since it is rare for powerboaters to enter this area. The first 100 yards of the right/north side of the creek are home to the monotonous, invasive species *Phragmities australis.* However, the shoreline quickly becomes pristine and the vegetation increases in lushness and diversity. All around you, minute variations of land elevation become apparent, with jewelweed giving way to river birch and then dipping back down in elevation to cattails and pickerelweed. There are several active wood duck boxes as you make your way up the creek. If you are kayaking in the autumn, you will often scare up a flock of waterfowl as you turn the early bends of the waterway. About 1 mile from the mouth, on the third major bend of the creek, you will pass a small grass clearing on your left with a cement block shed that is known as White Oak Landing. The landing is owned by Merkle Wildlife Sanctuary, which protects the entire southern shore of the Mattaponi (Patuxent River Park protects the northern shore). This is the best place to get out to stretch your legs or eat lunch. It has dependable dry land and you create no negative impact by going ashore here. Passing by White Oak and pausing there on the return trip is a good alternative if you paddled straight from Selby's into the Creek.

Whenever you do stop at the landing, you will notice a dirt road leading up the hill. Follow this road for a short hike to the sanctuary's observation tower. Walk up the dirt road to an intersection with another dirt road and take a left. Follow for about ¼ mile and then take a left to the lookout tower (there is a sign). Walk another ¼ mile to the lookout tower, which is several stories high and offers an unparalleled perspective of the surrounding area. The winding paths of Broad Creek and of Weir Creek can both be clearly seen. This is my favorite lunch location, for the tower's lookout is better than the view from any restaurant I know.

After White Oak Landing, the creek bends to the right, flows for a brief straightaway and then bends back to the left. At this left bend, if you look to the right you can glimpse the Mattaponi on the other side of the hairpin meander that you just completed. There is an osprey nest in a dead tree at this point, along with a large pile of gnawed timber which marks the edge of some beaver territory (this type of pile is locally known as a beaver scent post). From this area up, the right (northern) side has one continuous beaver dam, with several beaver lodges secreted away behind it. Paddling away from the beaver scent post, you will make a right, after which you will paddle under a wooden bridge that connects Patuxent River Park to Merkle Wildlife Sanctuary. The bridge is for pedestrian traffic only, except for Sunday afternoons, when it is open to the public as a Critical Area driving tour. This can be a nice place to stop and walk around; the view from the bridge is beautiful and offers the kayaker another bird's eye perspective of the route. There is a small pullout spot about 40 feet before the bridge, and then

Muskrat, River Otter, Beaver and Nutria

The Chesapeake is a subtle place. Just as our shorelines are intricate landscapes of low-slung marshes and forests, our semi-aquatic water mammals are quiet and stealthy. Though small and elusive, the bay's muskrat, river otter, and beaver are intricately tied with our ecosystem and have helped shape our streams and shorelines. To catch a glimpse of one of these shy creatures is a rare and special treat, a gift that is given mostly to the quiet boaters who rise at dawn, stay until dusk, and paddle on the silent overcast and rainy days that keep less intrepid kayakers indoors.

Muskrat are the smallest of the bay's water mammals, measuring a maximum of 15 inches long, with a narrow head streamlined with its lean brown body and thin, scaly tail. When you spot a muskrat it is usually on the move, slicing purposefully through the water with just the crown of its head showing. The muskrat eats primarily aquatic plants, however it is versatile and also dines upon small mollusks, crustaceans and amphibians. Their lodges can be spied on the edges of marshes. These homes are small mounds, averaging about three feet in height, and are constructed entirely out of grasses with an underwater entrance burrowed into the muddy riverbank. The muskrat has several litters of pups a year and the underwater entrance protects the brood.

River otters are the most secretive of the bay's mammals and are rarely seen by even the quietest of kayakers. They were completely extinct on the western shore due primarily to habitat loss and water quality degradation. Thanks to better land management and a re-introduction program, otters can once again be found on both sides of the Chesapeake. They are much larger than muskrats, usually 2½ feet long, with a thick furry muscular tail that tapers at the end. Like all of our bay mammals, the river otter is primarily brown and somewhat silvery white on its belly and chest. Their dens are in the marsh banks, with less of a pronounced mound than the muskrat den, but with the same type of underwater entrance. They are carnivores, hunting fish, amphibians, and crustaceans. Otters are intelligent and playful animals; I once spotted a

again directly before the bridge—just be sure to not disturb the marsh vegetation of the area. In order to paddle past the bridge you need to be kayaking at high tide. In the summer, even at high tide, your way can be blocked by a thick growth of Eurasian watermillifoil, an invasive submerged aquatic vegetation (SAV) that first became noticeable in 1999.

After the bridge there is an osprey platform on the right. The parent birds can become quite agitated if you linger, particularly if you pair at Gunpowder Fall sliding down the icy bank and splashing in the freezing river. What had been a rather bleak and bitterly cold paddle was transformed into my favorite trip of the winter.

Beavers are about the same length as the river otters, but with a longer face and fatter body. They are considerably less shy than the otter, and like muskrats, they are most often spotted while plowing across the river, only swimming below the water's surface when startled or entering their lodge. Their larger size and distinctive broad, flat tail easily distinguishes them from muskrats. Their habitat is the easiest to spot, due to their prodigious dam building ability. The purpose of these structures of mud and wood is to form a pond with a stable water level, behind which they can build a lodge out of a large pile of logs and mud with an underwater entrance that will never be exposed by tides or drought. The beavers' main food source is the nutrient-rich inner bark of trees. They can be inquisitive, but once the beavers have spotted and investigated you they will often disappear suddenly with a resonant slap of their tail, letting all beaver around know that you are there.

There is a fourth, non-native mammal of the Chesapeake and it warrants mentioning. Nutria are native to South America and were introduced to the Chesapeake Bay in the 1930s for trapping and fur production. Their fur did not find a market and they have exploded in population. They have the same vegetarian diet as the muskrat, but eat twice as much and devour the whole plant including the root structure, and in the process are carving up large swaths of marshland on the eastern shore. They have a skinny tail like a muskrat, but measuring at about twenty-five inches they are much larger than a muskrat and smaller than a beaver. Nutria have not become a visible presence yet on the western shore, so if you do spot one notify the Department of Natural Resources (DNR) so that they can keep tabs on the movements of these critters. The nutria is definitely a cautionary tale of the dangers in introducing non-native species to an ecosystem. *—A.N.*

are part of a large group. Respect the birds' home by not coming too close to their perch and continue on around the bend to the right, after which the creek ends at an expansive beaver dam. The dam has been there for decades and is strong enough to stand on, and by doing so you may be able to glimpse the large beaver lodge about 30 feet behind the dam. If you look past the large pond to the trees on the far shore you will notice one tree that is larger than the others and covered with what looks to be large balls. This tree is home to a great blue heron rookery, and the large balls are the heron's nests. Many herons can be seen throughout the beaver pond and the surrounding area.

The trip up the Mattaponi and back is a total of 4 miles (from the mouth of the creek). It is an easy paddle for beginning kayakers and I have spent all day in the creek, swimming, hiking, and just poking about. However, the Mattaponi can also be combined with trips into nearby creeks, such as Lyon's, Weir, and Broad Creek. To reach any of these creeks from the mouth of the Mattaponi, take a right and paddle river right—it is important to stay out of the main boat channel. Powerboats are not thick around here, but this section of the river is popular with water skiers and they can appear quickly from around the river bend. As you paddle farther downriver you will pass the osprey nest at the southern end of the Mattaponi's mouth. Continuing on for about ½ mile you will come to a point where the river makes a major bend to the right. To paddle into Lyons Creek, continue straight across the river at this point toward the far bank. Or, you can continue around the bend to head toward Weir or Broad Creek.

If you crossed the river to Lyons Creek, take a left once you reach the opposite shore and the creek's entrance will lie directly in front of you. There are some houses and piers in the beginning of the paddle, but they disappear as you head up the narrowing water. The shoreline becomes primarily forested, with higher banks than you experienced on the Mattaponi. At the first major bend to the right you will kayak over the site of America's oldest shipwreck, a 17–25-foot boat carrying at least 40 cannonballs and other munitions. The wreck is not visible since it is buried under many feet of sediment, but the fact that such a deep draft vessel was once able to navigate this waterway will give you an idea of the extent to which this creek has silted up over the years. The waterway is navigable for at least 1½ miles from its mouth, depending on the tide, and its forested banks provide some nice shade on a hot summer afternoon.

If you stayed on the right bank of the river when rounding the bend of the Patuxent, you will come upon the entrance to Weir Creek in about 100 yards. It is a small entrance to a creek, which is simply a bending slice in the surrounding marsh. One-third mile past Weir the Patuxent bends sharply to the right and you will find the entrance to Broad Creek in another ⅓ mile. Broad Creek runs through the same expanse of tidal freshwater marsh as Weir, but is more substantial. About 80 yards upstream of the mouth the creek forks, with the main waterway bearing left (west) and a smaller wandering gut to the right. Traveling up the main branch, you will come to another fork after about the same distance, with two equal creeks dividing the waterway. There is not much solid land for climbing out on, so you will have to appreciate this area entirely from your kayak as your own secret water garden of wonder. I paddle into creeks like Weir and Broad simply because I can, because I am a kayaker, and it seems like since I can fit into these little valleys of marsh and bear witness to the beauty then I should do exactly that. Solitude is your ultimate destination in these little creeks that go nowhere.

8. *Jug Bay and the Western Branch of the Patuxent*

> **Length:** 10 to 12 miles, depending on how much you explore Jug Bay. This trip could also be combined with the Mattaponi Creek to add more mileage and beauty to your paddle.
>
> **Put-in Site:** Patuxent River Park, Selby's Landing. An annual special use permit is required which can be purchased at the park office or by mail for $5 for residents of Prince George's and Montgomery Counties or $10 for noncounty residents. The phone number for the office is 301-627-6074 and the mailing address is 1600 Croom Airport Road, Upper Marlboro, MD 20772. There is a port-a-john at the landing. The park is open from sunrise to sunset. Maryland–National Capital Park and Planning Commission (M–NCPPC) manages this facility. Jackson's Landing is located by the office and places you above Jug Bay and nearer to the Western Branch.
>
> **Driving Directions:** From I-95/495, take Exit 11A, Pennsylvania Avenue S/E (MD 4) and follow for about 8 miles and then exit onto US 301 South, for about 2 miles. (An alternate route is to take US 50 to US 301 South and follow for about 15 miles, to

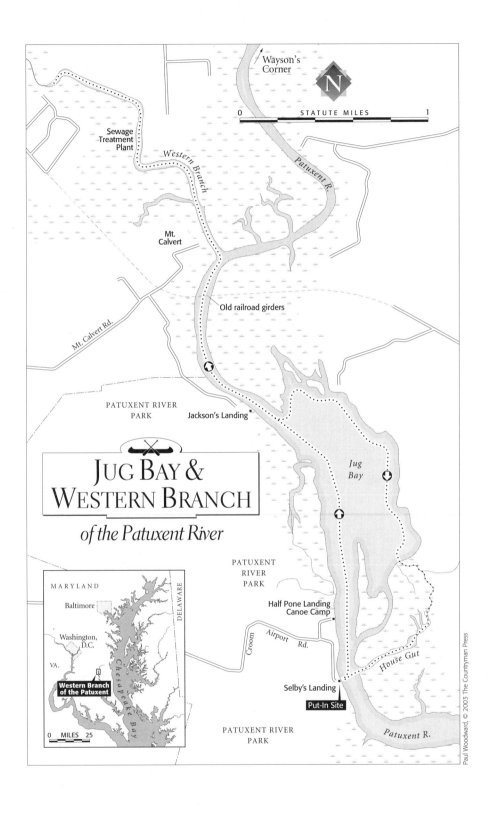

Wayson's Corner

N

STATUTE MILES
0   1

Sewage
Treatment
Plant

Western Branch

Patuxent R.

Mt.
Calvert

Old railroad girders

Mt. Calvert Rd.

PATUXENT RIVER
PARK

Jackson's Landing

*Jug
Bay*

JUG BAY &
WESTERN BRANCH

of the Patuxent River

PATUXENT
RIVER
PARK

MARYLAND

Baltimore

DELAWARE

Washington,
D.C.

VA.

Chesapeake Bay

**Western Branch
of the Patuxent**

0   MILES   25

Half Pone Landing
Canoe Camp

Croom

Airport Rd.

House Gut

Selby's Landing

Put-In Site

PATUXENT RIVER
PARK

Patuxent R.

Paul Woodward, © 2003 The Countryman Press

the junction with MD 4, and then use the rest of the directions as written.) Take a left on Croom Station Road and follow for 1.6 miles. Take a left on Croom Road (MD 382) and follow for about 1.5 miles. Take another left on Croom Airport Road (there should be a Patuxent River Park sign on the right-hand side of the road). Follow this road until it ends, continuing straight after the park entrance toward the group camp area (if you need to buy a permit, you should turn right at the sign for the park office before continuing on to the landing). At the end of the road, fork left toward Selby's Landing. The road ends in a small parking lot and the boat landing is at the bottom of the hill.

THE TRIP through Jug Bay and up the Western Branch of the Patuxent is a beautiful paddle through tidal freshwater marsh and riparian forests. But it is also a voyage through history—up an old working river and past the remains of railroads and plantations. The trip begins at Selby's Landing, which is the site of the first African-American owned airport in the United States. John Greene, Jr., and his aviation group, called the Cloud Club, opened and operated the center as Columbia Air Center from 1941 to 1958, with a brief interruption when the Navy commandeered the field for training World War II pilots. The airfield was the only place African-American pilots could train, and it was home to some of the most daring flying of its day, gaining a reputation for producing skilled stunt pilots and aviators. The wrecks that resulted from this relentless pursuit of skill are still scattered in the surrounding woods, where they were dragged because it was discouraging to other pilots to see airplane carcasses on the field. Patuxent River Park was formed in 1959, forever preserving Selby's Landing as a piece of U.S. history.

Paddling Notes

Paddle around the fishing pier and head to the left to begin your journey upriver. In about 100 yards the river widens into the area known as Jug Bay. This open pan of water was formed when the river skipped a meander, flowing straight overland and drowning the marsh-lands in its way. Due to this, the center is shallow, but the occasional speedboat captain still finds the channel, so sticking to the left edge is a good policy. The eastern (right) shoreline can be fun to explore, how-ever since it loops so far away I usually save this exploration until the end of the trip to ensure that enough time is left before the park closes at dusk.

A few yards after entering the open area of Jug Bay you may be able to spy the narrow opening in the marsh grasses that leads to the park's canoe campsite. This is a great home base for river explo-rations. Reservations fill up quickly however, with the park office being inundated with reservations on January 2 of every year, so plan ahead.

When kayaking on Jug Bay, while you want to avoid the center, be wary of traveling too close to the western edge unless you want to ex-perience the thick river mud intimately. The western shoreline is marsh of varying width, backed by the forests of Patuxent River Park. It is lush habitat and there is a heron rookery in the trees, near an observation platform that is only accessibly from land. The expanse of Jug Bay draws to a close about 1½ miles north of Selby's Landing, where you will pass Jackson Landing, the park's other boat launch. This landing runs from the back of the park office and is also where recreational kayaks can be rented. It can be used as a launch for this paddle, and will shorten the trip by about 3 miles.

Upstream of Jug Bay, as you travel on the slow bend of the river you may notice thick plastic mesh netting that has been installed here, and further on up the Western Branch, in an effort to limit the damage that the new resident geese population is doing to the grasses. The Chesa-peake's ecosystem evolved around a transient geese population. Our marshlands are not hardy enough to tolerate the year-round feeding of flocks, which have been lured into slothfulness by the excess of corn that is left on the farm fields every fall. About ⅔ mile past Jackson's you will float past the cement foundation of the center pivot point girder for a swing drawbridge for the Chesapeake Beach railroad, which con-nected Washington, D.C. with the booming resort town in the early to mid-1900s. On the right side of the river is the wooden platform that marks the other side of the railroad and is now owned by the Jug Bay Wetlands Sanctuary, an Anne Arundel County Park.

One mile past Jackson's Landing you will come upon Mount Calvert, a brick mansion set upon a high bluff at the confluence of the Western Branch with the main stem of the Patuxent. Bear left into the Western Branch, and then land on the beach at the base of the sloping grass-covered hill. Walk the grounds and enjoy the view from this beautiful estate. The land was acquired by the state in 1995 for 1.2 million dollars and is now a welcoming spot for kayakers and landlubbers alike, even providing port-a-johns for the civilized kayaker with a small bladder. Soon there may be even more facilities, as the manor house is being restored and archeological digs are being made in the surrounding land. Mount Calvert was the area's first land grant (granted in 1657 by Cecilius Calvert (Lord Baltimore) to his nephew Philip Calvert). In the 1680s the city of Charles Towne was founded there, and was the county seat of Prince George's County, until Upper Marlboro unseated it in 1721. The town disappeared and for the next 250 years the land was primarily farmed as a tobacco plantation. The courthouse, built in 1698, was converted into the plantation manor, with further additions added on in the 1800s.

After resting your muscles at Mount Calvert, point your kayak to the left and head up the Western Branch where the river flows between banks of lush freshwater marsh. Numerous guts cut into the western and eastern marshes that create the shoreline of the first 1 mile, and all are great places to explore. This habitat is lush and great for beaver, muskrat, wetland birds, and turtles. After a major bend to the left and then back to the right, you will pass a small landing on your right known as Iron Pot landing (about 1 mile from Mount Calvert). After another bend to the left, the river straightens and narrows with forest replacing marshland, dappling the water's surface with shadows. On days with a western breeze you may begin to notice the scent of chlorine in the air. After the ½ mile straightaway you will round the bend to the left and the source of the chlorination is revealed as the Western Branch Sewage Treatment Plant. On most days, the water from this pipe is cleaner than the silty Patuxent, and is so clear that great schools of fish can be seen in the depths.

The Western Branch continues all the way into the town of Upper Marlboro, which used to be a port town for shipping tobacco from the surrounding farms. Tobacco is a tough plant on the soil, and over the years the topsoil erosion from the tobacco plantations has filled in the river so much that it is barely passable for even kayaks. I have made the length of the trip and parts of it are like a lost world, with beaver swimming in the sunlight and a heron rookery suspended in the trees over the water. However, the going is rough due to multiple portages over fallen trees, and I would recommend bypassing this challenge and instead using your extra time and energy exploring the eastern shore of Jug Bay. This shore is quiet and shallow and you will find plenty of mummichogs flopping in the shallows with their faithful stalker the great blue heron never far behind. When the tide is high, at the southern end of the bay you will find a slough that will lead you into House Gut, which winds its way through the marsh until it empties into the river opposite of Selby's Landing. It is an enchanting way to end this beautiful paddle.

9.   *Upper Patuxent River*

> **Length:** The trip is about 24 miles. Unlike most high mileage trips, you will likely never see a powerboat for the duration of your trip and the water will remain flat and navigable in even high winds. While this is written as a there-and-back trip, the distance is considerable and the water in the upper section of this trip can be fast running in the spring or after a heavy rain, so you may want to consider setting up a shuttle. For a shuttle trip, you can use the Patuxent Wetland Park described in this trip, and take out at Selby's Landing. Or, to arrange for a downstream trip, you can make arrangements to launch upstream at the 4-H Center or the Queen Anne Bridge fishing area by calling 301-627-6074 or at Wooten's Landing by calling 410-741-9330. As usual, much less mileage can be paddled by just poking about—I wasted away wonderful hours floating around in this river's many side guts.

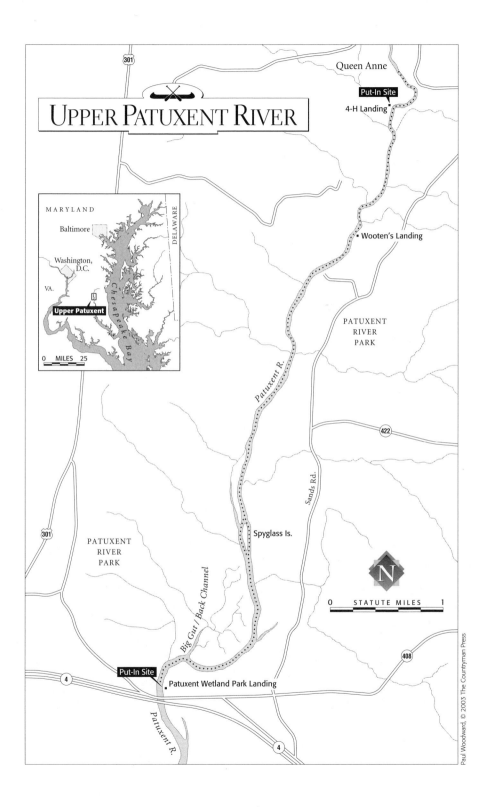

UPPER PATUXENT RIVER

Queen Anne

Put-In Site
4-H Landing

MARYLAND

Baltimore

Washington, D.C.

VA.

DELAWARE

Chesapeake Bay

Upper Patuxent

0   MILES   25

Wooten's Landing

PATUXENT RIVER PARK

422

Patuxent R.

Sands Rd.

301

PATUXENT RIVER PARK

Spyglass Is.

N

0   STATUTE MILES   1

Big Gut / Back Channel

408

4

Put-In Site
Patuxent Wetland Park Landing

Patuxent R.

4

Put-in Site: This is a small kayak landing and no fee or permit is required. There is ample parking, but no other facilities such as bathrooms. The launch point is up a 50-foot-long, shallow-water side gut. There is a wooden dock for fishermen where the gut joins the river, so be aware of their lines as you head onto the main waterway.

Driving Directions: From US 301 or I-495, exit onto MD 4 South. Two miles from US 301, exit onto MD 408 for Wayson's Corner/Annapolis. Take a left at the end of the ramp, cross back over MD 4 and then take the second left (the first left would put you on MD 4 North) into the Wetland Park. A large brown sign marks the road. Follow until the road ends at the landing; parking is by the launch and alongside the paved road by the launch.

THE PATUXENT RIVER has been my classroom, as a teacher and a student, for longer than any other waterway. I have included three trips along its shores, and could have easily included more, and not just because of my natural bias toward its shores. It is, on average, the deepest river in Maryland, and with a total length of 110 miles, it is the only river on the western shore whose watershed lies completely within the state of

The Upper Patuxent as it broadens at Wayson's Corner

Andrea Nolan

Maryland. It is a river that is firmly entrenched in Maryland's history and culture, and is in essence a mirror of the Chesapeake Bay in its ecology, politics, and natural and cultural history. After its humble beginnings as a small spring at the junction of Howard, Montgomery, Carroll and Frederick counties, the river is little more than a trout stream, slowly growing in strength and depth before being dammed by the Triadelphia Reservoir and then the Rocky Gorge Reservoir (which provide a combined 50 million gallons of drinking water a year). One mile below MD 214 the river's navigable section begins in earnest as the river drops into the flatter coastal plain. This is where the domain of the sea kayaker begins, and is the subject of this trip description.

Paddling Notes

When launching your kayak you need to head to the left to reach the Patuxent—at extreme low tides you may have to scoot along mud for a few feet before there is enough water to float your boat. Once on the Patuxent I recommend heading to the right and paddling upstream first, since this section can be the more strenuous if the upstream current is strong. Within the first ¼ mile of paddling you will see the entrance to two guts, the second one being locally known both as Big Gut and as Back Channel. It is a great side trip for poking around in, and is the northernmost tidal freshwater marsh on the Patuxent.

As you head upstream, the river gradually narrows and is surrounded by beautifully wooded bluffs with just a narrow margin of marsh vegetation creeping along the shores. For the next 3 miles, the western side of the river is protected by Patuxent River Park. On the right side you will pass a landing and pier for a trailer park that commands a scenic view from the hilly shoreline. You will pass Spyglass Island, which is generally navigable on both sides of the island, 1½ miles upstream of the landing. The water's depth becomes increasingly shallow as you head north and the river's bottom changes from mud to firm gravelly sand. Between the trees, you will occasionally see and hear the heavy equipment used in mining the gravel and sand pits that stretch along the hills of the eastern shoreline.

Andrea Nolan

The idyllic upriver passage of the Patuxent River

About 2 miles from the trip start you will pass Wooten's Landing, which has low slick mud banks and an outflow pipe (½ foot in diameter) discharging clean water from a small sewage treatment facility. This is a good site for getting out and stretching your legs, with plenty of dry land available for a restful lunch or snack. Wooten's Landing is one of the largest mitigated wetlands on the East Coast. The 72 acres of wetlands in the 140-acre park were planted to repair land that was damaged by years of use as a sand and gravel quarry. The restoration is the product of a joint 10-year effort by United States Fish and Wildlife Service, the Army Corp of Engineers and Anne Arundel County. A short hike up the broad trail will lead you past the treatment facility and up the hill to an observation platform that overlooks the sanctuary. There are numerous studies of the area being made to determine if this man-made area will function as well as a natural wetland, and none of these marked study sites should be disturbed. For the young at heart, there is a rope swing overhanging the water, and just past this is an inlet into a small pond. Your kayak may scrape bottom a bit getting into this meditative spot, but it is worth the scratches. After another peaceful 2 miles up the river you will come upon the small 4-H Center canoe landing on the left bank. This landing, like Wooten's, can be used as a launch site by planning and calling ahead.

After the 4-H landing, the tide's current begins to be overpowered by the river's southern flow, making it difficult to continue to paddle upstream when an ebbing tide combines with the river's own downstream current. However, if you continue 1 mile further upriver, you will come to Queen Anne Bridge, which is a decaying, early 1900s steel truss bridge that replaced a mid-1700s bridge in the same location as the main connector between Anne Arundel and Prince George's County. Queen Anne Town was built in the early 1700s and was a seaport from then until the mid- to late 1800s, which is hard to imagine on what is now a shallow, narrow and tree canopied river. The settlement is now known as Hardesty so as not to be confused with Queen Anne County, on the eastern shore. The bridge was crumpled by a heavy truck in the late 1940s and is now managed by Patuxent River Park as a fishing recreation area. This could be used as a launch area, but the banks are steep so great care is necessary to use this area. Contact Patuxent River Park for information.

If the ebbing current is strong, you may be able to enjoy the rare free ride on moving water as you head back downstream, but with your more rapid pace you need to be alert for any "strainers" created by fallen trees. While the current may not seem too strong, even a 3-knot flow can trap your boat if caught broadside against an obstruction. The section between Queen Anne's and the 4-H center can also vary in depth, and at times your kayak may scrape bottom.

The trip from the put-in to Queen Anne's is 16 miles and is more than enough for most paddlers. However, there is more paddling available downstream from the Patuxent Wetland Landing for those with the time and the energy. You will see some houses along the river's edges, but most of the surrounding area is protected by Patuxent River Park. The river broadens and is predominately marshlined. About ¼ mile south of MD 4/Hill's Bridge, on the western shore is Green Landing, which was the head of navigation on the Patuxent for 60-foot, ocean-going steamboats from 1878 to 1885, until the river became too silted in for deepwater vessels. The Marlboro Hunt Club now owns the property.

During this section of the journey, your kayak is coasting above a piece of United States history. During the War of 1812, Commodore Joshua Barney set fire to his Chesapeake flotilla of 17 ships in order to prevent their imminent capture by British warships. They now lie buried on the river bottom beneath more than 5 feet of silt. Despite this defeat, Barney was a highly successful naval officer, engaging more British ships in battle than his famous counterpart John Paul Jones.

About 1½ miles south of Hill's Bridge, the river widens as it bends to the west, with the eastern shore of this bend known as Pig Point, after the low-grade pig iron that used be shipped by this once busy port. Like all of the industry on the upper section of the Patuxent, Pig Point's dockyard was closed due to the extensive siltation from the surrounding tobacco fields. As you follow the river's flow to the west, there are several creeks flowing into both sides of the river. North Glebe Marsh to the left (south) contains plenty of muskrat habitat and beautiful marshlands on both of its branches. On the right-hand (northern) side, Railroad Creek and Monday Creek also provide some fine poke-boating opportunities.

About ¼ mile past Monday Creek you will pass the mouth of the Western Branch with its distinctive Mt. Calvert house perched high upon the bluff. Selby's Landing is another 2½ miles downstream from here. A detailed description of this area is provided in the Western Branch trip description. The length from the put-in at Wayson's Corner to Selby's Landing is about 5½ miles, for a round trip of 11 miles. Combined with the upstream portion of this trip you have a total of 27 miles of water to cover, not including side trips. There is definitely enough water here for several day trips. Since side explorations are part of the joy of the journey, you should definitely paddle this area repeatedly to cover all the possible routes in the navigable reaches of the upper Patuxent.

10. *The Spa Creek to South River Marathon*

Length: The route described is about 24 miles. You can easily round up that mileage to a marathon-length 26 miles by exploring any number of side trips. A shuttle trip, of half the length, is possible by leaving a second car at Quiet Waters Park and pulling out at the Amphibious Horizons boat dock (see contact info in the appendix). Or, you can paddle just a section of this area, creating your own poke-boater's journey.

Put-in Site: The launch is the boat landing in Truxton Park, a city recreation area located on the headwaters of Spa Creek. There is a beach next to the powerboat ramps that is a perfect launching site for kayaks. There is no fee for non-trailered boats launched from the beach and there are bathroom facilities in the parking area.

Driving Directions: (From Baltimore take I-97 South or from Washington take US 50 East.) From US 50, take exit 22 which is Arris T. Allen Blvd./MD 665. Stay straight on MD 665 (DO NOT bear to the right onto Riva Road). After about 1 mile the road name changes and becomes Forest Drive eastbound. Stay straight on

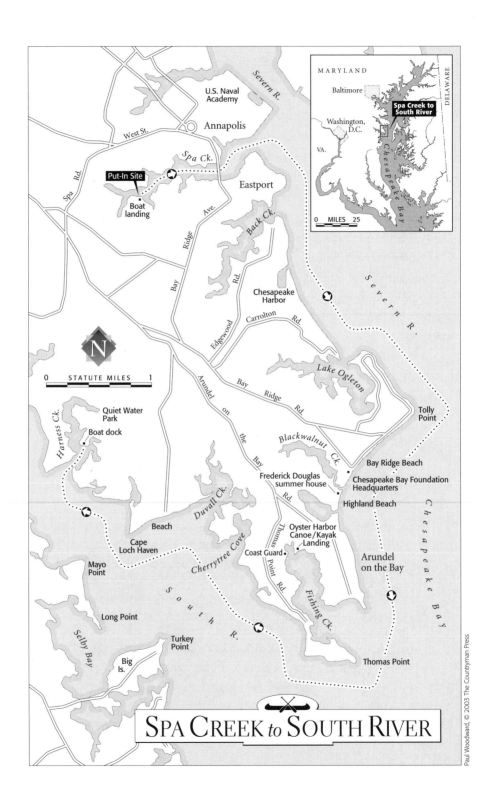

Paul Woodward, © 2003 The Countryman Press

Inset Map

Main Map

U.S. Naval Academy

Severn R.

Annapolis

West St.

Spa Ck.

Spa Rd.

Put-In Site

Boat landing

Eastport

Back Ck.

Ridge Ave.

Bay Rd.

Chesapeake Harbor

Edgewood Rd.

Carrolton Rd.

Severn R.

N

STATUTE MILES

0   1

Lake Ogleton

Arundel on the Bay

Bay Ridge Rd.

Tolly Point

Harness Ck.

Quiet Water Park

Boat dock

Blackwalnut Ck.

Bay Ridge Beach

Chesapeake Bay Foundation Headquarters

Frederick Douglas summer house

Highland Beach

Duvall Ck.

Beach

Cape Loch Haven

Cherrytree Cove

Oyster Harbor Canoe/Kayak Landing

Coast Guard

Thomas Point Rd.

Arundel on the Bay

Chesapeake Bay

Mayo Point

South R.

Fishing Ck.

Long Point

Selby Bay

Turkey Point

Big Is.

Thomas Point

SPA CREEK *to* SOUTH RIVER

Forest Drive and then take a left onto Hilltop Lane. Go straight through the intersection with Spa Road. In about 1 mile, take a left on Primrose. Follow that road into Truxton Park, following the signs to the boat landing, bearing right at a split in the road. There is room on the big turnaround by the ramps to temporarily park for unloading your kayaks and gear. Parking is about 50 yards up the hill from the water.

THE CITY OF ANNAPOLIS is the capital of Maryland, home to the United States Naval Academy and is the city I live in and love. Somewhat swayed by affection for my hometown I have included two Annapolis-based trips, one in the downtown waters as well as this trip that transverses all the surrounding waters of Annapolis. The reason for the double dose of Annapolis extends beyond the purely sentimental and rests upon the very geography and history of the area. Annapolis is a city of 30,000 on a peninsula that is one of several that create a greater peninsula that contains the extended city of another 70,000 residents. This larger peninsula is formed by the Severn River and the South River, with the bay offering the boundary at the tip of the land mass. Since the majority of Annapolis's kayakers live in the greater Annapolis area, we do much of our paddling outside of the downtown area. The visiting paddler should paddle where we paddle to truly experience our town. The open water, expansive vistas, and marathon length and populated shorelines create a route that differs from most of the trips in this guidebook. Wind generated waves and powerboat wakes can create ocean-like conditions more similar to the coastal waters of California and New England than the sleepy tidal creeks of the Patuxent or the Blackwater, therefore this trip is intended for experienced paddlers.

Paddling Notes

When launching from Truxton Park, downtown Annapolis is to the north on your left and Eastport is to the south on your right. The South River is south of Spa Creek, so paddle alongside the southern (right) edge of Spa Creek to avoid having to cross over its wide mouth when it meets with the busy Severn River. For more detail about the surrounding shoreline see the next trip description on Annapolis proper. In about a ½ mile you will paddle under a drawbridge, past the harbor of City Dock to your left and in another ½ mile you will round Sycamore Point, bearing to the right to head southeast on the Severn River. There are often a large number of sail and powerboats moving around in this area, so stay relatively close to shore. As you paddle southeast, the 5-mile-long double spans of the Chesapeake Bay Bridge are to your north. A ¼ mile further south you will pass Back Creek. This is the first of a multitude of creeks, coves, and ponds that punctuate the shoreline of this trip. Some specifics about Back Creek can be found in the Annapolis trip description, however, for the sake of brevity I do not provide details on the majority of these side-routes. They are all short waterways, and all contain still waters and hidden secrets—it is up to you to decide which ones to explore.

South of Back Creek you will pass the inlet of little Chesapeake Harbor, and then the communities of Sparrows Beach and Annapolis Roads, which includes a public golf course. Excellent swimming beaches characterize this area and will be with you for the duration of your paddle. Most of these beaches are owned by the local community

Mike Savario

Author Andrea Nolan, second from left, practicing rescues in Hanover Creek with instructor staff

associations and maintained for their residents' use. The large majority of these beaches, and their users, are friendly and welcome the passing kayaker; just respect the residents' rights, make sure to land your boat out of the way of swimming kids and clean up any trash that you create. Several beaches have large nets surrounding them in the summer months. These are jellyfish nets, and even at high tide you should not paddle over these highly valued community resources.

After passing over the broad opening to the cove of Lake Ogleton you will spend the next 2 miles paddling by the scenic shores of Bay Ridge. For ½ mile you will pass by a beach that is segmented and protected by a multitude of jetties. Upon rounding Tolly Point, your direction of travel will shift from the southeast to the southwest and you will officially enter the Chesapeake Bay. At the point, the beaches drop away as the shoreline steepens into a cliff, whose base is buffered by a line of riprap. As quickly as they rise, the cliffs descend and with their loss reappears the beach, with the next ½ mile protected by riprap sea walls. Bay Ridge has long been used as a summer community for residents of Washington D.C., however with today's fast cars and highways most of the homes are now year-round residences. The architecture still retains a breezy summer cottage character, and tucked in between three-story new homes you will still see small bungalows with wraparound screen porches. At the end of the sea-walled beach, you will pass a building that dwarfs the neighboring homes. It is the Chesapeake Bay Foundation's headquarters and is a pioneer building in energy conservation and land use, the perfect base for an organization that has spent the last 30 years fighting to "Save the Bay."

Immediately after the narrow, windy inlet for Blackwalnut Creek (which I highly recommend poking around in), the next beach and community that you will pass is Highland Beach, which was established in 1893 by Major Charles Douglass, the son of former slave, author, and abolitionist Frederick Douglass. Major Douglass purchased the land after he was denied service at a nearby Annapolis restaurant, and he designed and built it as a 44-acre beach resort. The first house you pass at the beginning of the community's ½-mile-long beach is the home that Charles built for his father. Frederick Douglass died before the house was completed, but was pleased with the building site, stating, "As a free man I could look across the Bay to the land where I was born a slave." Like in Bay Ridge, all of the homes are set back across the road from the water, opening up the beach for use by the entire community. Many of the original residents' descendants still live in Highland Beach, making this community the country's oldest African-American resort community.

After Highland Beach, you will pass the inlet for Oyster Creek and then you will be traveling along the shores of Oyster Harbor and Arundel on the Bay. Unlike Bay Ridge and Highland Beach, these communities are relatively newer and many homes are built directly on the waterfront, limiting public access. However, there is a small Oyster Harbor community beach immediately after the inlet and the Arundel on the Bay community beach is a ½ mile further on around the point and facing Thomas Point Lighthouse and the broad opening for Fishing Creek.

You will have been able to see Thomas Point Lighthouse for much of your trip. Since it lies 1 mile offshore of Fishing Creek, this is the best place to leave from in order to get a closer look at this working landmark. It is the only Chesapeake Bay screwpile lighthouse still in use in its original location, and it is a distinctively beautiful building with a hexagon shape, white clapboard siding, black lantern, and red tin roof. (Screwpile lighthouses were developed by Alexander Mitchell, a blind Irish engineer and brickmaker, in 1833. The metal pilings screw deep within the mucky bottom, allowing for solid construction even on such densely muddy bottoms like those found throughout the Chesapeake Bay. Built in 1875 and automated in 1986, Thomas Point was the Chesapeake Bay's last staffed lighthouse.) The excursion out to the light is only for experienced paddlers who are confident in the weather and their skills; all others should admire it from a distance. You must be extra vigilant for passing powerboaters; they are rarely expecting or looking out for kayakers as they speed along in the open bay. If you wish to paddle inland, Fishing Creek is an interesting diversion with the Annapolis station of the U.S. Coastguard at its headwaters, along with the Oyster Harbor kayak landing a little to the north of the station with

Andrea Nolan

The Bay Ridge beach is protected by riprap

some picnic tables available for a comfortable lunch. It is a 2-mile round-trip detour into the creek.

The tip of the southern side of Fishing Creek is Thomas Point and while it is a public park, it is not a receptive place for kayakers. The small beach on the South River side is exclusively for fly-fishermen and other than that, the rest of the shoreline is comprised of riprap. South of Thomas Point is the broad mouth of the South River; swing your bow right to head upstream and into the final 3-mile leg of the "there" section of this paddle. On any weekend day from May to September the river is a busy place with dozens of powerboats moving at a rapid speed, producing considerable swells and breaking waves as the result of their wakes sloshing back and forth in the relatively narrow river. The South River is statistically the most dangerous and fatal river in Maryland, which is entirely due to powerboat collisions. That danger is easily avoided by staying well clear of the channel and by never crossing the river on a weekend day.

As you head upstream, the woods of Thomas Point will fade away and be replaced the estates of Thomas Point Road. After passing Cherrytree Cove you will cross the broad mouth of Duvall Creek, which is

Jellyfish

Jellyfish are those strange stinging globs that haunt our bay waters and terrorize unaware swimmers with their prickly venom. The fact that the Chesapeake has numerous nonstinging jellyfish means nothing to most bay area residents; for us jellyfish and the stinging sea nettle are synonymous and we use the names interchangeably. The more colorful description of sea nettle comes from the quality of the jellyfish sting, which is similar to the pricking of nettles in a forest. The sting isn't dangerous for most people and the intensity of prickling lasts for only a half hour before leaving behind a red patch that may last a little while longer. Our jellyfish are benign when compared to the venomous punch of the man-o-wars of the open ocean. However, they are ours and so it is best to know a few things about the swimmer's nemesis.

Sea nettles can grow to be as large as 7 inches across with tentacles hanging up to 2 feet below the bell. The stinging portion of the jellyfish is the nematocysts, which are found in the goo of the tentacles. The nematocysts are microscopic darts which lodge in your skin, so when stung you should first scrape off the area as best as possible—a credit card works well, or while in a kayak I have used the blade of the paddle or the edge of a laminated chart. After scraping, rinse the area clean with bay water. Fresh water would further aggravate any remaining nematocysts. After taking these measures I usually let time do the rest, but if you or your patient is really uncomfortable, vinegar can diffuse the sting, as will your own urine (someone else's urine is a bit unhygienic and *ooky*).

It is important to remember that sea nettles aren't out to get us—we just happen to get in the way of their travels. They are plankton, which means that they can move vertically through the pulsing of their bell, but any horizontal movement is at the mercy of the current. Their sting is intended to shock small fish that swim into their tentacles. Once stunned the fish are eaten by the ruffled mouth, which is at the base of the body. If you get lucky you can sometimes spot an undigested fish inside of a jel-

home to the friendly community of Hillsmere. The mouth of Duvall is wide, but if you are alert to in and outgoing boaters you can cross the expanse safely. The Hillsmere public beach is on the northern side of the creek. There are several community boat landings and piers within the creek's branches.

After Duvall Creek, you will pass the small inlet to Hillsmere's pond, and then, after a few more houses and gently curving, tree-lined shore, you will come upon a pair of small weathered wooden seawalls lyfish. Everything in the jellyfish is visible through its translucent skin, including its reproductive organs which can become darker mid-summer. You can astound your friends by identifying the sex of the jellyfish—male gonads are white or pink, female parts are olive.

While telling a sea nettle's sex is a good trick, the real talent comes in safely picking up a jellyfish. To accomplish this feat, grab the jellyfish by its bell. Since all of the nematocysts are on the tentacles, the bell can't harm you. To further wow the crowd, with a flat hand with fingers pressed together, stroke your palm down the length of the stinging tentacles. The skin on the palm of an adult's hand is too thick for nematocysts to penetrate so you will not be stung; children's hands are generally too soft to protect them, so they should not try this maneuver. Besides being an interesting trick, this skill comes in handy when swimming because you can now remove them from your harm's way. Bay kayak instructors are quite practiced in doing this prior to any of their students performing a wet exit. However, remember that you can only remove the jellyfish that you can see. Long pants/running tights with socks are your best protection against submerged sea nettles. To avoid inadvertently stinging yourself, rinse any goo off your hands after handling jellyfish in order to remove the nematocysts.

While sea nettles may be annoying, they are a part of the bay's ecosystem. Jellyfish are the primary food for many species of sea turtles and even dolphins enjoy them as a good snack, both of which are nomadic visitors to the lower bay's salty waters. Sea nettles are unlike anything else in the bay and I enjoy their mysterious beauty. However, if you are still not a fan of the sea nettle, pray for rain. They need salty water, so a drought will produce more jellyfish than a wet year. They are particularly sensitive to winter moisture amounts. Their northernmost range is Annapolis, where they arrive as early as mid-May and as late as mid-August. They always disappear before the trees have changed color in the fall. —A.N.

protecting the entrance to Loden's Pond. This quiet sanctuary is definitely worth exploring. At different times I have seen red fox, deer, bald eagle, blue heron, and river otters in this shallow and serene little cove. Past the entrance to Loden's is Quiet Waters Park, and the first "facility" that you will encounter is the dog beach and sea wall. Kayakers are also welcome to land on the far end of the beach, away from the sea wall. For an excellent view, walk up the path on top of the sea wall and up the cliff's stairs to the two white gazebos overlooking the water. You can reach some very civilized flush toilets by walking about a ¼ mile up the paved trail. Quiet Waters Park is an Anne Arundel County Park with 5 miles of paved bike trails, numerous picnic pavilions, a summer outdoor concert series, art gallery, and a sculpture garden.

Continue exploring the park by paddling past the seawall and into Harness Creek. As you travel, stay a little ways out from the seawall; the combination of shallow water, boat wakes, and the hard wooden shoreline can create some considerable clapitus (rebounding waves) capable of dumping even the most experienced paddler. Once you are in Harness Creek you will see the Amphibious Horizons rental boat docks on the northern shore. You are welcome to land on the low kayak dock; just make sure to keep your boat out of the way of the launching and landing rental boats. This is a pretty creek with houses on one side and forested parkland on the other. Two coves and the narrow headwaters provide some still waters for watching blue herons and kingfishers. However, do not linger too long, because unless you have left a shuttle car here, you still have 12 miles to paddle before reaching the finish line and completing your paddler's marathon.

11. *Annapolis*

> **Length:** The combination of every route in this trip is an ambitious 20 miles with two open water crossings. However, you can easily omit the open passages to lessen the mileage. The beauty of Annapolis is available with even a 3-mile trip.
>
> **Put-in Site:** The launch is the boat landing in a city recreation area, located near the headwaters of Spa Creek, known as Truxton Park. There is a beach next to the powerboat ramps that makes a perfect launching site for kayaks. There is no fee for boat-carrying cars and there are outhouses in the parking area.
>
> **Driving Directions:** (From Baltimore take I-97 South or from Washington take US 50 East.) From US 50, take exit 22 which is Arris T. Allen Blvd./MD 665. Stay straight on MD 665 (DO NOT bear to the right onto Riva Road). After about 1 mile the road name changes and becomes Forest Drive eastbound. Stay straight on Forest Drive and then take a left onto Hilltop Lane. Go straight

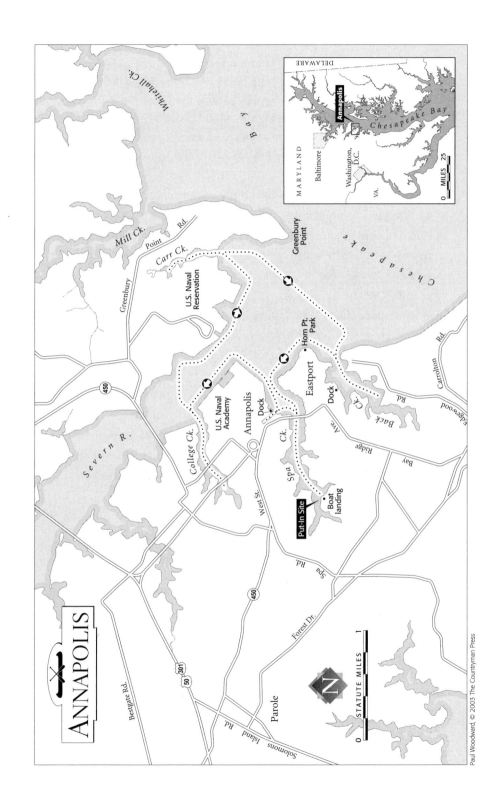

ANNAPOLIS

Whitehall Ck.

Bay

Mill Ck.

Point Rd.

Carr Ck.

Greenbury

U.S. Naval
Reservation

Greenbury
Point

Chesapeake

Severn R.

College Ck.

U.S. Naval
Academy

Annapolis

Dock

Horn Pt.
Park

Eastport

Dock

Back Ck.

Carrolton Rd.

Edgewood Rd.

West St.

Spa Ck.

Bay Ridge Ave.

Put-In Site

Boat
landing

Spa Rd.

450

Forest Dr.

50 301

Bestgate Rd.

Parole

Solomons Island Rd.

450

N

STATUTE MILES

0   1

DELAWARE

MARYLAND

Baltimore

Annapolis

Chesapeake Bay

Washington,
D.C.

VA.

0   MILES   25

Paul Woodward, © 2003 The Countryman Press

through the intersection with Spa Road. In about 1 mile, take a left on Primrose. Follow that road into Truxton Park, following the signs to the boat landing, bearing right at a split in the road. There is room on the big turnaround by the ramps to temporarily park for unloading your kayaks and gear. Parking is about 50 yards up the hill from the water.

PADDLING THE SHORES of Annapolis is not a wilderness experience, but instead provides a unique beauty all its own. Annapolis has a subtle grace devoid of dramatic skyscrapers or huge monuments. The city is steeped in history, with 18th-century brick and clapboard houses lining the streets and creeks creating a waterscape that is one of the most beautiful in the world. Overlooking this colorful landscape is the white wooden cupola of the State House, which sits on a high hill and is visible through much of your journey. This distinctive building was built in 1772, was used by the Continental Congress between 1783 and 1784, and is still home to Maryland's legislature, making it the oldest state capitol in continuous use. Annapolis is a water town—most residents live, work, and/or recreate on the water. While the favored form of recreation is sailing, many are discovering kayaking as an economical way to get onto the water. With both sailors and landlubbers joining the kayaker's ranks, the sailing capital of the East Coast may be soon known as the kayaking capital as well.

Paddling Notes

When leaving the beach of Truxton Park you will be in the headwaters of Spa Creek. To paddle to the head of navigable water you should bend around to the left. The left (northern) shoreline of the creek is entirely made up by Truxton Park's wooded shoreline. Spa Creek splits into two equal branches, which end in about a ¼ mile. The left branch ends by a low pedestrian bridge connecting Truxton Park to the neighboring houses. The right branch travels under a unique serpentine footbridge that you can glide under at low tide, to eventually reach the head of the creek which terminates at a beaver dam. Paddling downstream from

City dock, downtown Annapolis

Truxton you will have the shores of Eastport to your right (south) and Annapolis to your left (north). While Eastport is officially part of Annapolis, it is very much a distinct neighborhood. In 1998 it "officially" declared its independence in a drunken revolt on Super Bowl Sunday, thereby becoming the Maritime Republic of Eastport (the independence day is celebrated with an outdoor party and tug-of-war in late autumn). Eastport has a history every bit as lengthy as Annapolis, at one time sheltering Lafayette's troops and for many years serving as the shipbuilding center of the middle bay. The shoreline covenants of East-port require all businesses to have a distinct maritime purpose. Many boat manufacturers, sail-makers, and other niche marine industries still operate out of the Maritime Republic.

On the left shore are the streets of historic Annapolis, which are lined with beautiful homes, mostly built in the late 1700s and early 1800s. After the grounds of St. Mary's Catholic Church and School you will pass under the drawbridge that connects Eastport to Annapolis, and then wrap around the edge of the Annapolis Yacht Club to paddle into the heart of Annapolis. The narrow harbor is a no-wake zone, however you still need to be alert because in the summer months there can be dozens of boats moving at any given time, all of which will be considerably larger than you. You may see several tour boats that operate here from spring to autumn, including the *Woodwind* schooners, which dock to the left of the entrance, and the large steamship *Harbor Queen,* which docks to the right. Annapolis's narrow inlet is affectionately known as Ego Alley after the tendency of boaters to parade up and down the stretch showing off their polished crafts. It can be fun to join the parade in your kayak, but watch for the mild whirlpools and eddies that are created by the churning propellers.

The City Dock of Annapolis lies at the head of Ego Alley and is available for dinghy docking. (Kayaks are included in this category.) Depending on the tide, the dock can be 2 feet or higher above the water surface, so be sure in your balancing abilities because you will have a sizeable audience eager for the entertainment of your capsize. To the left of the dock is a statue that represents Alex Haley reading from his book, *Roots*, about his ancestor Kunta Kinte who was sold as a slave on this very dock. Directly across from the dock is the Market House, which has a variety of booths selling sandwiches, baked goods, and seafood. I recommend Sammy's Deli's massive sandwiches for the hearty appetite. The area around the City Dock is filled with restaurants, coffee shops, and the local favorite, Storm Brothers Ice Cream shop. The Harbor Master, a Visitor's Center booth, and public rest rooms can be found in the center kiosk of the parking area that lines the northern (right) side of City Dock.

Often moored by the dock is the Chesapeake Bay Foundation's educational skipjack, the *Stanley Norman*. The boat's current captain is an avid kayaker himself, so give the crew a wave if they are aboard; just don't interrupt the teaching. Upon leaving Ego Alley, bear to the left and push a bit away from shore to stay out of traffic. Paddling in the midst of the mooring field is a relatively safe enterprise and you can often meet friendly sailors from around the world as you glide past their yachts. To your left you will be passing the impressive campus of the U.S. Naval Academy. There is no place to pull ashore so if you want to visit the academy grounds you must do so by tying up at City Dock. The copper rotunda that is visible during much of the trip is the academy's chapel. The U.S. Naval Academy is home to 4 thousand midshipmen who are a visible presence around Annapolis.

The seawall of the academy makes a 90-degree bend to the northwest, signaling your departure from Spa Creek and your entrance into the Severn River. The Severn is active with sail- and powerboats, so paddle near shore but a little distant from the seawall to avoid rebounding waves. In about ¾ of a mile you will reach the calm waters of

Back Creek's sea of masts

Andrea Nolan

College Creek, which can be a fun place to explore, with three bridges and a footbridge to paddle under. The Naval Academy owns both sides of the creek's mouth, with the midshipmen's rowing dock and boathouse located on the northern shore. After the last bridge, the southern (left) shore belongs to St. John's College and you will see their boathouse and dock. St. John's was founded in 1696 as King William's School and is the third oldest college in the United States. Francis Scott Key and a nephew of George Washington were two early alumni. Since 1937 the school's curriculum has been based on the great books of Western civilization, where students learn to read the ancient works of literature in the original Greek.

After College Creek it is possible to continue paddling upstream on the Severn for many miles. You will see the first of two Severn River bridges lying about ½ mile to the north of College Creek. Another mile above that is Weems Creek, and above that is the larger bridge, which services US 50. However, my suggested route is to cross the Severn River at College Creek and then paddle back downriver. A naval station occupies the eastern tip of the shoreline, and after passing the navy's boat basin you can enter Carr Creek for a pretty paddle amongst forested shorelines. This is still government land, so don't come ashore—the shooting range is to your left and the creek ends at the naval station golf course.

Leaving Carr Creek, you will have to pick your way across the mouth of the Severn River, which is about 1 mile wide at this point. Due to the high amount of boat traffic on this convergence of the Severn River, Spa Creek, and the Chesapeake Bay, you must be sure of your paddling skills to make this crossing. If you are not confident paddling in confused seas, with high and frequent boat wakes, then you should never cross over to the northern side of the river. However, for a competent paddler this open water crossing can be fun to bounce across. Straight across from Carr Creek is Horn Point, the northern point of the mouth of Back Creek. This creek is the backyard of Eastport and it is an interesting paddle beside the sea of sailboats in the boatyards and marinas that line the shore. McNasby's seafood market, cafe, and museum can be seen about ¼ mile up the creek on the East-

Summer Squalls

The rapid heating of land by 90-plus degree temperatures and humid, moisture-laden summer air creates localized thunderstorms that we call squalls. These brief and intense storms, with high winds, thunder, and lightning occur almost every summer afternoon somewhere on the bay; the unknown and unpredictable factor is where the squall will be on any given day. While providing a dazzling show, thunderstorms are frightening to experience in the open bay, so watch for signs of an incoming squall, periodically monitor your weather radio, and save any open water crossings for the calm morning hours.

Usually you can tell a squall is coming when a bank of clouds creates a dark line that generally moves north and northeast across the water. You can often spot them when they are more than an hour away, but this can vary, particularly if you are paddling in a forested river with limited visibility. You need to develop your weather sense, which is mostly a matter of experience: watching the clouds, noticing wind shifts, and gauging fluctuating temperatures. Pay attention if you notice that clouds are bunching up into the fluffy clouds of cartoons. These clouds could continue to pile up into cumulonimbus clouds, which are thunderheads. Buy a book and teach yourself how to read cloud formations.

While squalls usually move in a northeastern direction, weather patterns do not always follow the rules, so pay attention to which way the wind is blowing and to the storm's movement. Squalls tend to track over waterways and will even follow boat channels. I once stood completely dry on an island and watched a storm pass 50 feet away from me as it followed the buried riverbed of the Pocomoke Sound. One effective way of tracking a storm is by counting the time between the flash of lightening and the boom of the thunder. It takes 5 seconds for the sound of thunder to travel a mile, so if you count 25 seconds between the flash and the boom the storm is 5 miles away. If the next flash and boom are closer together then the storm is heading your way.

If a squall is coming, make for land. My rule of thumb is to be off the water when the lightning is less than 3 miles away, so gauge how long you have before the squall will be that close and then paddle toward the best refuge you can reach within that time. Once on land, the safest outdoor location is within a grove of trees, making sure you are not under the tallest tree. If possible stand inside of a 45-degree angle from the trees' crowns to keep away from the roots. (This is called the "Cone of Safety.") If there are just a few trees in a clearing, you should steer clear since they will attract lightning. Often in the Chesapeake you will be on open marsh. Sit on your life preserver, because this will protect you from any ground currents and also make you a small target. Stagger your group out in the marsh, so that if the worst does happen only one person will be hit. Once settled, put on your rain gear and enjoy the show. Most of our squalls last little more than 45 minutes. If the land is too marshy to get into, stay in your kayak with the bow wedged up onto shore. Be glad your kayak is not made of metal and enjoy the fireworks. —*A.N.*

port/right side at the end of Second Street and Annapolis Sailing School is on your left. You can tie up your kayak at the dinghy dock, which is at the end of Sixth Street, past the boat slips and marinas. The water is shallow and the wall is high, so you will get your feet wet stepping into the river and climbing up the ladder to the street above. From here you can wander the peaceful streets of Eastport and visit one of the pubs or restaurants that are scattered about this tiny peninsula.

After Back Creek, paddle northwest back up the Severn and around the tip of Eastport. Horn Point Street End Park is visible at the end of Chesapeake Avenue and has a nice sandy beach for landing your kayak, providing a good alternative to the Sixth Street dock. Fort Horn once sat on this spot, and housed Maryland militia, General Lafayette, and his French troops in the Revolutionary War. Prior to the bridge, you will see a large warehouse on your left with a sign that reads *Backyard Boats*. Poke your nose in here and you will find a small floating dock with a rack of assorted kayaks on the parking lot above it that is owned by Springriver, the local kayak shop. You are welcome to land your kayak to pay the store a visit; just be sure to move it out of the way of any launching or returning rental boats. The store is in the front of the building and the Springriver crew is a friendly bunch with a ton of expertise. They also rent kayaks, so this can be your launching spot for the day if you are traveling with people without their own boats.

Once you have finished gawking at the latest and greatest kayaks, take a left from Springriver and paddle a mile up Spa Creek to reach the landing at Truxton Park. I highly recommend making your way back downtown by car and digging into some crab cakes and oysters for dinner at one of the downtown restaurants. The best part of a long paddle is often the guilt free feast that can follow.

12. *Gunpowder Falls*

Length: The trip mileage is easily increased or decreased, but is 12 miles if all options in the paddling notes are covered.

Put-in Site: Mariner Point Park in Joppatowne. This area is managed by Harford County Parks, and their contact number is 410-612-

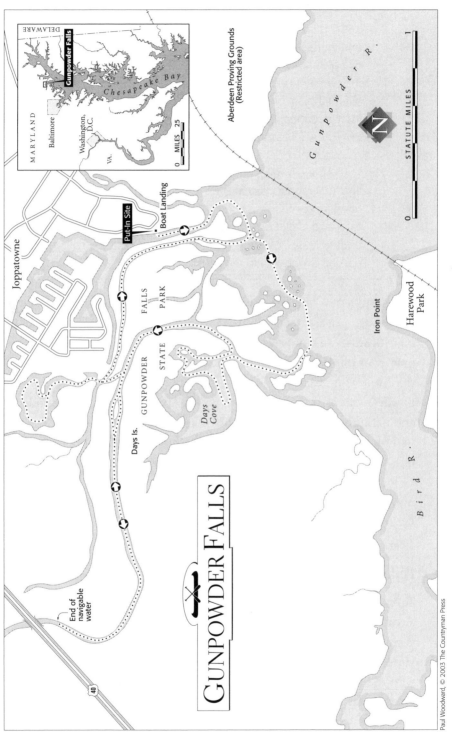

GUNPOWDER FALLS

1608. It is open from 7 AM to 8 PM, there are no launching fees, and there are bathroom facilities. The ramps are heavily used by powerboaters, so be sure to unload you gear to the side of the turn around. The boat landings are on Taylor's Creek, a short tributary of the Gunpowder.

Driving Directions: From I-95 Northbound (above Baltimore) take exit 67A/43 East/White Marsh Blvd., bearing right. Follow this road to a long exit ramp; at end of ramp bear right to US 40 East. After 4.5 miles take a right on Joppa Farm Road at a traffic light (a shopping center is on the right). Follow Joppa Farm Road for about 2 miles through a residential neighborhood and then take a right onto Kearney Drive. Follow for .5 miles until it ends in Mariner Point Park. The boat landings are on the right, parking is in the lot to the left.

WHILE THE WORD "FALLS" conjures up harrowing images of cascading whitewater, rest assured that this section of Gunpowder Falls is the domain of sea kayaks, not river rafts. The river's namesake lies many miles upriver of this tidal section; only the hair-raising name continues with the river. More than any other trip on the western shore the Gunpowder, with its location between US 40, Aberdeen Proving Grounds, and Baltimore is wilderness disguised as an urban paddling site. Even with the surrounding metropolis, the river reigns supreme—in very little time a kayaker will find scenery that is as wild as anything that can be found in more remote areas. Opportunities to explore abound, as more than 12 miles of sloughs, guts, ponds, and rivers wrap around 5 square miles of land.

Paddling Notes

Take a left at the put-in site and paddle south along the western edge of Taylor's Creek to allow plenty of room for passing powerboaters. Once you reach the mouth of the creek the powerboats part company with kayaks and continue out into the open bay, leaving the upriver waterways to the intrepid paddler. The wide river in front of you is the main Gunpowder River, mostly created by the confluence of the Gunpowder

Falls and the Bird River. A towering railroad bridge spans the water, and in the distance the distinctions of the riverbanks fade into the open bay. The shoreline downriver to the left is the Army's Aberdeen Proving Ground and is off-limits to any shore wandering. The land to the right is all privately developed.

Swing your bow to the right and head upriver past a long and shallow cove that has been carved out of the marshland. What at first glance appears to be impenetrable marsh is actually several islands with the narrow sloughs between them, providing numerous shortcuts to the main river. This early into the paddle I am rarely looking for a shortcut and prefer to save them for the trip downstream. However, for those with time or physical restrictions, a fun hour can be spent weaving your way amongst these sloughs. Once past all the side guts of the cove, you will pass the mouth of the main stem of the Gunpowder Falls. While unremarkable in size, the water flows rather determinedly through this opening and is unmistakable as a primary flow. As tempting as this water is, I like to extend the open water traverse a little longer and continue past the Falls with the green marsh on my right and the open water and railroad to my left.

About 1 mile after you leave Taylor's Creek you will come to a small point of land, which for the last eight years has been marked by a duck blind. There is a small slough on the upriver side of the point that has enough water to float a kayak. Here I finally yield to the temptation of the shortcut into what is a broad gut. This gut is the second part of the main flow of Gunpowder Falls and you should bear right (east) to head upstream. If you miss the shortcut, the wide water of the Bird River will come into view in front of you and you will see the gut's large opening in the marsh on your right. The only difference is that now you are paddling on the west side of the delta island, while the shortcut was on the east side.

In about ½ mile you will come to the small entrance on your left that leads to Days Cove. While expansive, it is shallow and in some sections of the cove even a kayaker could run aground. It is a wonderful place to explore, for no wrong turns can be made. There are scattered marsh islands in the center, a forested shoreline all around, and intermittent dry land sites along the shore for stretching your legs or eating lunch. It is possible to waste away an entire afternoon in this gentle cove.

After Days Cove, take a left to continue upriver and you will soon join up with the main stem of Gunpowder Falls. Here you can take a left to paddle upstream, or if you are out of time, you have two options for heading back to the landing. My preferred option is to paddle straight across the river, then head upstream for about 6 strokes, which will take you to a small gut on your right. This shortcut empties into the broad cove you passed on the way out, where you can hang a left to head back to the launch site. If the water level is low, or you are leery of a shortcut, paddle to the right on Gunpowder Falls and follow it back into the open water of the main Gunpowder River. Once there, take a left and head back to the launch.

If you are up for more exploring, there is still plenty to do and see on this forested river. Paddling upstream (bearing left) you will journey through lush marshland on relatively broad water that is generally devoid of anyone but the occasional kayaker. You are now in the midst of urban wilderness. About 1 mile upriver from Day's Cove you will pass an island midstream, which has good break spots on its right side. There are some shallow spots around here, but you can push past them and the river will deepen again. On a hot day, this is also a nice place to get out to wade and swim, since the bottom is mostly firm gravel and the water flows clear and cool.

Past the island, houses that may have occasionally blinked into view will disappear from sight, the marsh fades away, and the river becomes a broad avenue of water flowing through the woods. This mile of water is one of the most enchanting sites on the bay's western shore and I could paddle it over and over again. Eventually you will come to the end of navigable water, usually within hearing or seeing distance of US 40, depending on the tide. Above US 40 the river moves into some elevation, defeating any tidal flow and all paddling is a one-way trip and not quite suitable for sea kayaks.

When you return downstream, you can take an excellent side route back to the landing via the Little Gunpowder Falls. The cut-through to the Little Gunpowder Falls is on your left and is barely ⅛ mile past the island. It is easy to miss, so stay sharp. Once you have cut over you can either swing right to paddle downstream, or head to the left, while bearing slightly to the right, to enter into a fun little pond with gravel islands in the center and civilization along the shore. Little Gunpowder Falls veers off to the left of the pond and I have not explored it, always finding it too obstructed with fallen trees to be navigable.

One of the things that you will likely notice on your way down the Little Gunpowder Falls is the prevalence of large wooden bird boxes on poles planted in the water and marsh. On almost any tidal river you paddle in the Chesapeake you will come upon these boxes, often built with two boxes back to back, each measuring 2x1x1, with round hole openings and slanted hinged roofs. These are wood duck boxes and were built as a substitute for the ducks' preferred habitat in the hollowed out cavities of old, dead, or diseased trees. Since mature riparian forests with decaying trees are scarce, their natural habitat has all but disappeared and the ducks were becoming endangered. However, the ducks have adapted to the boxes well and their population is making a comeback. These particular wood duck boxes were installed by Joppatown High School in partnership with the Chesapeake Bay Foundation. About eight years ago I took the group of students who installed them out in canoes to inventory and repair boxes—my first introduction to this beautiful river.

The Little Gunpowder parallels Taylor's Creek, the two waterways being separated by just a narrow strip of land. You will end up on the wide expanse of the Gunpowder River, where you can then take two quick lefts to head back to the launch. While the powerboats have been carving up the open bay, you have paddled a piece of urban wilderness known by very few people. Count yourself lucky to be a Chesapeake kayaker.

13. *Susquehanna River and Flats*

> **Length:** The total trip length, beginning at Jean Roberts boat landing, is about 20–24 miles, depending if you explore the is-

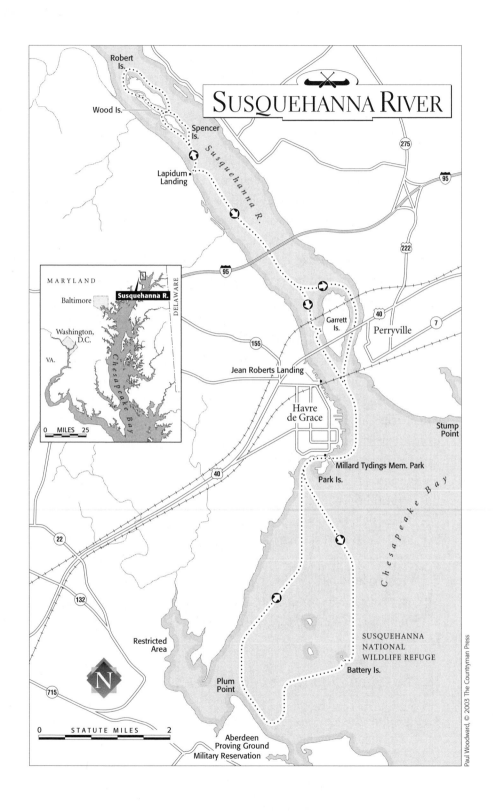

SUSQUEHANNA RIVER

Robert Is.

Wood Is.

Spencer Is.

Lapidum Landing

Susquehanna R.

275

95

222

95

Garrett Is.

40

Perryville

7

155

Jean Roberts Landing

Havre de Grace

Stump Point

Millard Tydings Mem. Park

Park Is.

Chesapeake Bay

40

22

132

Restricted Area

715

SUSQUEHANNA NATIONAL WILDLIFE REFUGE

Battery Is.

N

Plum Point

0   STATUTE MILES   2

Aberdeen Proving Ground Military Reservation

Inset map

MARYLAND

Baltimore

Washington, D.C.

VA.

DELAWARE

Susquehanna R.

Chesapeake Bay

0   MILES   25

lands upstream of Lapidum Landing. A vehicle shuttle works well in this area, and can reduce your distance to 15 miles if you launch at the Lapidum Landing (brief driving directions are provided in the paddling notes) and take out at Tydings Memorial Park in Havre de Grace.

Put-in Site: Jean Roberts Landing is my preferred launching point on the Susquehanna, and is a small boat landing with limited parking at the northern end of Havre de Grace, with a $5 fee on weekends and holidays. Warren Street is across the road from the landing, with the Starrk Moon Kayak retail and rental shop just visible from the landing.

Driving Directions: From I-95, exit on MD 155 East. This will intersect with US 40. Cross over US 40, onto Juniata Street. Take a left onto Otsego Street and follow until it ends at the boat landing.

To launch or leave a shuttle at Tydings Memorial Park, the other Havre de Grace landing, take a right onto Union Avenue at the end of Otsego Street. Follow until it ends and then go left on Commerce. The park is on your right, and the entrance is at the far end of the park (on the right). Fee is $5, to be paid at the marina office. There are bathroom facilities here. To reach the upriver Lapidum boat ramps, take the first left on MD 155 East after you exit I-95.

THE SUSQUEHANNA RIVER is a mighty force that provides more than 50 percent of the fresh water to the Chesapeake. It flows 444 miles from its headwaters in Cooperstown, New York, southwards through Pennsylvania until it finally empties into the Chesapeake Bay by Havre De Grace, Maryland. If you want to get right down to the science of it, the Chesapeake is essentially an extension of the Susquehanna, but received the separate name of Chesapeake due to its estuarine qualities. Buried beneath the shallow pool of the bay is the drowned river valley of the Susquehanna, which now serves as the major channel of navigation for large cargo ships. Maryland's state line crosses the river about 12 miles north of the bay, and it is tidal for the 8 miles southward from Smith Falls to the bay. Smith Falls is a shallow area of rock ledges, which marks the northernmost point of exploration by Captain John Smith in his tour of the Chesapeake. Generally the Susquehanna and upper bay flow fresh, but like all tidal parts of the bay, the waters can become brackish in times of drought. Several years ago the river became salty enough that a 12-year-old boy caught a small shark while fishing from Havre De Grace's riverfront, providing a vivid reminder that the Atlantic Ocean lies only 195 miles downstream.

Paddling Notes

Havre de Grace's name is French for "Harbor of Grace" and this picturesque little town perched on the top of the bay lives up to its name. Incorporated in 1785, its architecture and sleepy streets are reminiscent of that time. Jean Roberts boat landing is in the shadow of a railroad bridge, which spans the distance of the Susquehanna from the northern end of Havre de Grace over to the town of Perryville. While the pretty shores of Havre de Grace beckon, begin your trip by paddling upstream while your muscles are still fresh. Garrett Island is visible straight ahead of you and is a densely forested island that supports two bridges. The southern bridge is the Hatem Memorial Bridge with US 40 and the

Approaching the mouth of the Susquehanna

Mike Savario

second narrower bridge is for a railroad. Beds of SAVs generally surround the island and landing spots vary with the water level. The river depth is highly variable, with an 80-foot hole off the northern tip of the island. See the Perryville trip description for some history of the island and its bridges.

While the island is navigable on both sides, on either your way up or down you should stay on the western side to get a closer look at an impressive quarry operation. The quarry is operated by the Arundel Corporation and is commercially valuable due to its juxtaposition to the deep water of the Susquehanna River, eliminating the need for a railroad to transport rocks to ships. You can paddle pretty close to the shore for a good look at the barges and piers, but stay alert for any moving ships. You are definitely the little fish amongst some awfully large whales, so it is your responsibility to stay out of their way.

About 1 mile north of Garrett Island you will pass under the high bridge bearing I-95. The river's depth continues to vary wildly, so you need to watch for submerged rocks and pilings. The shoreline here is generally wooded and the water runs cold and clear. Susquehanna Park protects the shoreline and contains campsites and hiking trails farther upstream. Scan the tree line as you paddle; this area is home to a large number of bald eagles, especially in the winter months. Lapidum Landing's boat ramps are about 1½ miles north of I-95. You will likely notice a quickening and strengthening of the current as you near this landing, and on some days you may not be able to paddle any farther north. The current is entirely dependent on the amount of water being released from the Conowingo Dam, which is about 4 miles upstream. If the upstream current's flow is moderate, and you are confident of your paddling abilities, continue to head upstream to explore Spencer, Robert, and Wood Islands, which you can see about 1 mile above the launch. You can land on the riverbank opposite the islands in order to take a look at the old mill and shipping canal and the park's informative trailside information displays about the historical industries of the lower Susquehanna. Be alert for the many people fishing from the riverbank. On your return trip south, remember to watch for any submerged trees, rocks, and pilings. These obstructions can be more difficult to dodge if you are riding a fast current downstream.

Once you pass Jean Roberts boat landing and the last railroad bridge you will begin the 1-mile paddle along the scenic waterfront of Havre de Grace. You will have paddled about 8 to 10 miles, so to satisfy your lunchtime hunger, you may want to visit one of the many downtown restaurants, all of which are accessible by a short walk from Jean Roberts landing. The Tidewater Grill is on the waterfront just south of the boat landing, and if you are dining at the grill you can land on their beach. Havre de Grace ends at the mouth of the Susquehanna and is marked by the Concord Lighthouse which is one of the oldest lighthouses in continual use in the United States. As you round the point you will see a boardwalk that rims the waterway, and just prior to the marina you will pass the Bayou Hotel, with a commanding view of the Chesapeake Bay. Built in 1921, it is now privately owned condominiums. To reach the Tydings Park boat landings, bear right, in between the fenced Park Island and the boat slips. The landing is at the far end of the park. You can access the boardwalk from Tydings Park, and its pathway will lead you to the Decoy Museum, the Maritime Museum, and to the Concord Lighthouse. There are rest rooms at Tydings along with a small outdoor food concession that is open during the summer months.

The water below this area is known as the Susquehanna Flats and is generally shallow, with an average depth of 4 feet. This area is the delta for the Susquehanna and thus is the final depository of 444 miles of collected sediment. The channels of navigation cut close to land, on either side of the flats, so this is one of the few areas of the bay where it is safer to paddle in the open water rather than close to land. There is not much protection on the flats on a windy day, and a substantial chop can quickly develop, so keep that in mind before venturing out into the open water. However, on a calm day the exploration of this area can be quite peaceful. There are generally massive beds of SAVs here, and historically this area has hosted flocks of migratory waterfowl so dense that you could not see the water between the ducks. About 3 miles south of Havre de Grace is Battery Island. This small island is protected by Susquehanna National Wildlife Refuge and makes for a good desti-

Andrea Nolan

Havre de Grace boardwalk and Decoy Museum

nation for your open water crossing. Unlike the rocky Susquehanna islands, Battery Island is made out of the same sand that composes all of
the flats. There are good landing spots on all sides, but there is some
poison ivy in the interior of the island, so be vigilant.

For a change of scenery, paddle closer to shore on the return trip
to Havre de Grace, while still keeping well clear of the channel. To begin
the journey home, first paddle south, before turning to the west and
then north to come close to the shores of Aberdeen Proving Ground.
This area is restricted and under no circumstances should you land
your kayak—you not only could be arrested, but you could also
stumble upon unexploded bombs. However, by paddling offshore along
Aberdeen you can scan the tree line for the large population of bald eagles that apparently are willing to endure the noise of bombing for the
luxury of miles of undeveloped, forested shores and interior lands. In
the winter this area is host to almost two hundred eagles.

The Susquehanna is a paddle entirely unlike any other on the bay. It
is a fine combination of forest and sunshine, civilization and wilderness. If you did not explore Havre de Grace during lunch, make sure
you take the time to walk the scenic streets before you leave town.

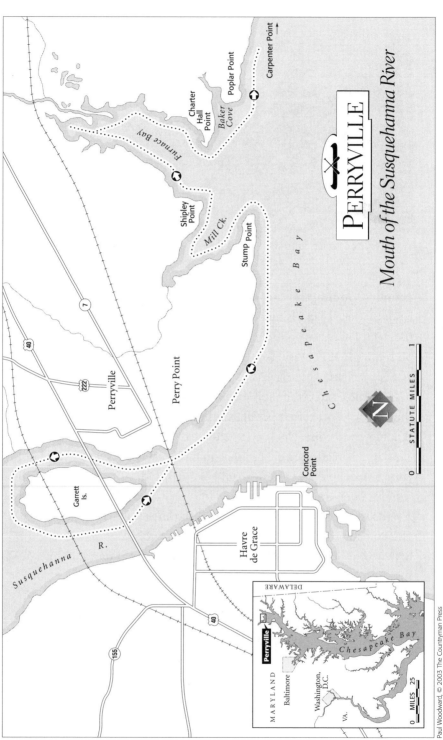

PERRYVILLE

Mouth of the Susquehanna River

Carpenter Point
Poplar Point
Charter
Hall
Point
Baker
Cove
Furnace Bay
Shipley
Point
Mill Ck.
Stump Point

Chesapeake Bay

7

40

222

Perryville

Perry Point

Concord
Point

Garrett
Is.

Susquehanna R.

Havre
de Grace

40

155

N

0   STATUTE MILES   1

MARYLAND
Baltimore
Washington,
D.C.
VA.
DELAWARE
Perryville
Chesapeake Bay
0   MILES   25

Paul Woodward, © 2003 The Countryman Press

PART II

Eastern Shore

14. Perryville/Mouth of the Susquehanna River
(Mill Creek, Furnace Bay, Susquehanna River, Susquehanna Flats)

Length: As short or as long as you like, but 5 to 10 miles depending on route.

Put-in Site: Perryville Community Park on Mill Creek

Driving Directions: From Annapolis follow I-97 north to route I-895 through the Baltimore Harbor Tunnel to I-95 north. Follow I-95 north across the Susquehanna River. Take the first exit after crossing the Susquehanna and passing through the tollbooth:

Mike Savario

The Blackwater River from Shorters Wharf in the Blackwater National Wildlife Refuge

Exit 93/US 222, Perryville/Port Deposit exit. (Stay in the right lane after the toll. Exit comes up quickly.) Follow US 222 across US 40 (pass through traffic light). Go to stop sign and turn left onto Principio Furnace Road/MD 7. (At the stop sign there is a small, brown sign pointing to the "Community Park.") Continue for .04 mile and turn right onto MD 327 east (no sign at this street corner, turn onto MD 327 east just past the Perryville Fire Company on the right). Continue another .03-.04 mile and turn right onto Tapp Parkway and you will pass under a sign for Perryville Community Park. From this sign to the put in is 1.4 miles (mark your odometer). Once in the park you will come to a "Y" or the first opportunity to travel left. Take this left and the black top will change to gravel. Keep traveling until your odometer reads 1.4 miles and park to the left of the road. As of this writing the put-in site is undeveloped, but should be quite user-friendly by summer 2004. You can put in here. Prior to this the bank is too steep.

ACROSS THE MOUTH of the Susquehanna River from Havre de Grace sits the small town of Perryville in Cecil County. Just south of the center of town is the Perryville Community Park where kayakers are allowed access to hundreds of acres of undeveloped shoreline, protected paddling, and views of rolling hills and cliffs as well as Garrett Island in the Susquehanna.

Paddling Notes

Like many of the trips described in this guide there is an abundance of paddling to be had here. Expect to spot eagles, herons, kingfishers, and large fish churning the bottom in the shallows. Since the Susquehanna River is the largest tributary feeding the Chesapeake Bay and supplies 50 percent of its fresh water, this entire area, although tidal, is a freshwater environment. Paddlers will enjoy a greater variety of vegetation here than in the saltier reaches of the Chesapeake.

From the put-in you have a tough decision: should you paddle left to the protected waters of Mill Creek and Furnace Bay or should you go right around Stump Point and paddle up the Susquehanna to Garrett Island? Or should you do both? Fortunately, any choice is excellent. Let's start by paddling left from the put-in and meander up Mill Creek. The entire shoreline is free from development. As you approach the top of Mill Creek, paddling becomes increasingly difficult due to shallow water. However, look for the channel and you may, depending on tide, be able to paddle up as the creek narrows. The area is a freshwater/riparian zone with a good deal of bird habitat. Not far up the narrow part of Mill Creek, your path will be cut short due to blowdowns.

From here turn around and begin to head out of Mill Creek on the opposite shore. I scouted this area in early May and the shoreline was rich with the blossoms of wild azalea and many other flowering plants as well as a lush carpeting of greenery.

If you follow the eastern shore of Mill Creek and round Shipley Point you will pass into Furnace Bay. Gazing southeast you view the rolling hills and cliff banks of Elk Neck State Park on the peninsula between North East River and Elk River that terminates at Turkey Point. The liquid world between you and the rolling hills is the beginning of the Chesapeake Bay. Furnace Bay is worth an exploratory paddle. Similar to Mill Creek, but larger, the shoreline of Furnace Bay is pristine except for one house on its southeastern tip. This bay offers decent, small, gravel beaches on its western side for rest and lunch breaks. It too gets shallow as you paddle to its source. Stay to the middle as you go and then to the eastern side where you will find a channel that allows access to Principio Creek at the head of Furnace Bay. Where Principio Creek meets Furnace Bay lies a pristine freshwater marsh. On the day I scouted this area eight great blue herons (see page 161) were stalking about searching for snacks. There is probably a rookery near by, so if you see a bunch of herons it may be best to stay clear to keep from disturbing them.

Leaving Furnace Bay you can continue along the shoreline heading southeast and experience floating on the open Chesapeake and eventually around Carpenter Point to explore the North East River. Expect to see more development and possibly increased boat traffic if you choose this path.

The other option on this paddle is to head right from the put-in spot, float out of Mill Creek around Stump Point and paddle up the Susquehanna River. You will pass a United States Veterans' hospital and several new buildings on the edge of Perryville. From here it is easy to see Havre de Grace across the river. Gaze up the Susquehanna and spot Garrett Island named after John W. Garrett who was the first president of the Baltimore and Ohio Railroad.

Prior to Garrett Island you will pass some piers that used to support the Philadelphia, Wilmington, and Baltimore Railroad bridge that was opened to traffic in 1855. In 1906 it was converted to pedestrian and vehicular traffic until the US 40 bridge opened. The first bridge you pass under on the way to Garrett Island is the Pennsylvania Railroad Bridge, completed in 1906, and built to accommodate the increased weight and size of trains. Amtrak currently uses it. The next bridge is the US 40 bridge that crosses the southern part of Garrett Island, and on the northern end of Garrett Island is the Baltimore and Ohio Railroad Bridge that was completed in 1886.

Garrett Island is undeveloped, pristine and beautiful. Keep in mind it is privately owned so be respectful and leave only footprints if you stop there for a break. The crossing from the eastern side of the Susquehanna to Garrett Island is less than ½ mile, but powerboat traffic is common. You could cross under cover of the US 40 bridge. Circumnavigating the island is a nice trek and you can make your way back to Mill Creek from there.

An interesting bit of history is that the northeastern part of the island was the location of a once thriving ice harvesting business. In 1875 icehouses were created to store the 100 thousand tons of ice being harvested from the Susquehanna. Huge saws were used to cut out ice blocks that were then hauled to shore by horse and stored in the icehouses. Layers of straw separated the blocks of stacked ice.

One other possible paddling spot is the Susquehanna Flats area. The flats lie just south of Stump Point. At low tide the water here ranges from ½ foot to 5 feet. At high tide the deepest area is 7 feet or so. With great caution the flats are a nice place to paddle at low or midtide since there will be little boat traffic in the shallow areas. Just keep an eye out and consult a chart to keep in the shallowest areas. There is a channel that stretches from west of Stump Point to Carpenter's Point to the east.

15. *The Upper Sassafras River*

Length: This trip can be any length you choose, and is an excellent location for novice paddlers because of its calm, protected waters and easy destinations. The full route, including Jacobs Creek, is 9 miles. Paddling around Hen Island and up Hen Island Creek brings the paddle to about 11 miles, or extending the trip to the bridge between Fredericktown and Georgetown creates a round-trip journey of about 15 miles. A portage possibility exists between Fox Hole Landing and Georgetown, which is about 3 miles away. That option is not described here, but could easily be plotted with local maps/charts.

Put-in Site: Fox Hole Landing is a small beach landing for carry-in boats like kayaks with no fee (there is no fee for kayaks at any Kent County Landing). There are no bathroom facilities at this landing. After unloading your vehicle, park along the side of the road.

Directions: From the western shore, take US 50/301 over the Chesapeake Bay Bridge and continue on US 301 when the routes split. Follow US 301 North past VA 213 and the first turn-off for MD 290 about 23 miles from the US 50/301 split). About 12 miles past the first intersection with MD 290 take the right exit onto MD 290 toward Chestertown/Galena. At the end of the exit ramp take a left onto MD 290 South. Go about 100 yards, and then take the first right onto Fox Hole Road. At the intersection with John Peel, continue to follow Fox Hole straight across. Drive down the hill and the road will end at the landing.

THE UPPER SASSAFRAS flows from east to west, with its navigable waters almost reaching Delaware. This journey takes the paddler into that uppermost section, where the river becomes narrow enough to step across. The brief description of this area mirrors its subject but belies the largeness of my affection for this unassuming trip. Few boats travel these peaceful waters, and I have seen bald eagle, fox, and deer all on

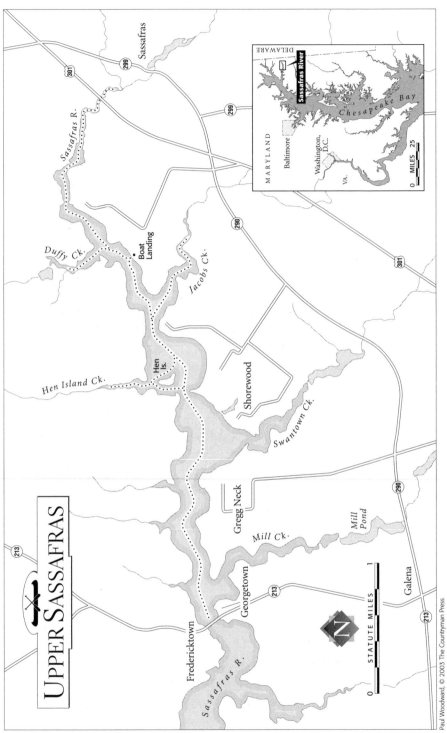

UPPER SASSAFRAS

Duffy Ck.

Sassafras R.

Sassafras

299

301

Boat Landing

Jacobs Ck.

290

301

Hen Island Ck.

Hen Is.

Shorewood

Swantown Ck.

Gregg Neck

Mill Ck.

Mill Pond

290

Georgetown

213

Galena

213

Fredericktown

Sassafras R.

213

N

STATUTE MILES

0   1

DELAWARE

MARYLAND

Sassafras River

Baltimore

Washington, D.C.

VA.

Chesapeake Bay

0   MILES   25

Paul Woodward, © 2003 The Countryman Press

one quiet afternoon. A large heron rookery can be viewed from the water, and is a sight that has paused my paddle for long, awed moments. This is a poke boater's paradise, with marsh, forest, creeks, and coves all devoid of human activity and aching to be explored. Birders and natural history buffs will be delighted, while people who crave a bit more nonstop paddling can extend their trip westward into the gradually widening waters of the Sassafras.

Paddling Notes

This trip is one of nosing your kayak into places that few people travel and striving for stealth as you sneak up on whatever wildlife you may have spotted on the shores. To start your trip with an amazing sight, paddle across the Sassafras to the small cove indentation on the opposite shore, to the right (east) of the green horse pasture and power lines. The water is shallow here, with thick mud that is often stirred up by large carp that are rolling and furrowing in the muck. While the carp are interesting, the real show is found in the tall trees on shore, which are home to an expansive and noisy blue heron rookery. There are usually more birds here than you can count, and the multitude of nests can be seen from the landing on the opposite shore. I would estimate the rookery population to be about one hundred birds.

After this raucous beginning, point your bow to the right and head upstream. Duffy Creek is a pretty little waterway that empties in from the north (left) in about 50 yards. I sometimes explore this side route on my way up the Sassafras, and sometimes on the return trip—just make sure you take the time to poke around within its shores. As you follow the Sassafras upstream you will pass a few piers on the right side before all signs of civilization ends. The left (northern) shore is lined with mature oaks, beeches, and pine trees, behind which are rolling hills of green fields and pastures. The majority of wildlife that I have seen on the Sassafras has been in this quiet section of water. The river steadily narrows and in about 1½ miles you will reenter the modern world as you reach the US 301 overpasses. Just prior to US 301 is a sand bar on the left-hand side, which despite some goose droppings can make for a dry, nonmuck rest stop before you make your way back downstream. You can hear the roadway, but the sound level is not too bad. Once under US 301, the creek splits. To the right is the Herring Branch and I have never found it to be very passable, but you may have luck at high tide. According to the chart, the water widens farther upstream so your efforts may be rewarded by a lengthy extension to your journey. The main branch of the Sassafras continues to the left, and in another ½ mile you will travel under the bridge for MD 299. There is another good snack spot just past the bridge, but the traffic noise is louder here. Beyond **MD** 299 the creek shallows and narrows, and very quickly becomes impassable.

When you paddle back downriver you will also notice a grassy rest spot on the left-hand (southern) side of the bank about ½ mile downriver from US 301, which is quite removed from any traffic noise. There

---

Killifish and Silversides: The Chesapeake Bay's Small Fish

Every Chesapeake kayaker will run aground as they explore the bay's side guts, edges, and flooded marshlands. Oftentimes you will discover that you have company, in the form of hundreds of small fish flopping and burrowing in the mud, thudding into your kayak, and occasionally ending up in your lap. The frenetic little fish are usually killifish or silversides. Since kayakers are some of the smallest boaters on the bay, it seems proper that we familiarize ourselves with the smallest fish.

Killifish are found on every continent but Australia and with their name "killi" meaning river in Dutch. They are the most prevalent minnow in the fresh and brackish water sections of the bay, and are divided into many different species according to their niche in the Chesapeake. Most are 2–4 inches long and are brownish green with rounded tails. They eat small crustaceans, worms and mosquito larvae, and killifish have been successfully introduced into ponds and streams for mosquito control. Mummichogs are a species that are found in the muddy shallows of freshwater rivers and the upper bay, and it is these hyperkinetic fish that are most likely to jump in a Chesapeake kayaker's lap. They are the chubbiest of the killifish, with pale silvery stripes, and form large schools. They were named for this characteristic, mummichog being a Native American word that means "going in crowds." Because of this trait, it is quite easy to cup your hand to scoop up a mummichog to take a closer look; just be sure to scoop some water up as well so that it can breathe.

The other common killifish the kayaker will see in the bay are the

is some poison ivy mixed in with the grass, so watch where you sit. The trip up and back, including the side trip of Duffy Creek, is about 5 miles. If you wish to extend your trip, about ¼ mile downstream from Fox Hole Landing, the Upper Sassafras's beauty is mirrored in the lazy wanderings of Jacobs Creek whose wide entrance can be found on the left (southern) side of the river. This slip of water slices deep into the earth, leaving high, forested banks that block out any view except for what is directly in front of or above you. As you near its headwaters, the shady waterway narrows so that it is little more than a stream. A deer once nearly hurdled the bow of a client's kayak as it jumped from bank to bank, startling them so much that they capsized in six inches of water—truly poke boat paddling at its best.

I have always ended my paddle after Jacobs; 9 miles can last a surprisingly long time while wandering about the Upper Sassafras. How-

---

banded, striped, and rainwater killifish. Banded killifish are often found swimming alongside mummichogs, but also can be found in brackish water environments. They have silver-blue vertical bands striping their sides, are much more slender than the mummichog, and are usually 4 inches long. The schools of fish swimming along the edges of sandy beaches are usually striped killifish, which look similar to mummichogs, but have dark vertical bands for the male and horizontal bands on the female. The smallest killifish in the bay is the rainwater, which only reaches 1 inch in size and has no stripes or other markings.

Silversides are long, shiny fish that live in the bay year-round and can range up into fresh water, although they are more commonly a saltwater fish. Like killifish, silversides are a valuable food source for larger fish and wading birds. The three species of silversides, the Atlantic, inland, and rough, are difficult to differentiate. All are slender, small fish with a shiny silver stripe running the length of their sides. The rough silverside can be seen in schools running in shallow water over sandy bottoms. The Atlantic silverside is slightly fatter and longer than the rough silverside and can be seen mixing with mummichogs in the middle bay, moving into the marsh to feed at high tide. I once came across a school of Atlantic silversides marooned in a marsh salt pan by the retreating tide, and they flashed and sparkled like a gleaming silver platter as they moved in unison in the morning sun. The glistening illusion was one of the most beautiful things I have ever encountered, and it was created by one of the bay's smallest creatures. —A.N.

ever, if you still have time and energy, you can continue to extend your paddle downstream. Hen Island is about ½ mile south of Jacobs, with the mouth to little Hen Island Creek directly to the north of it. Continuing further to the west will bring you past Swantown Creek and Mill Creek, both of which are as long as the beginning section of the Upper Sassafras. The bridge that connects Fredericktown to Georgetown is 3 miles to the west of Fox Hole Landing. This area is all ripe for exploring; just be aware that powerboat traffic will be increasing slightly as you enter the wider, deeper waters of the Sassafras. I am content to drift along the upper reaches of this hidden gem of the Chesapeake.

16. *The Sassafras River and Turner Creek*

Length: The route described, up Turner and Lloyd Creek, is 12 to 17 miles depending on how much exploration you do in Lloyd. Betterton Beach is 5 miles from the boat landing, on the mouth of the Sassafras, and for the strong-muscled and -hearted you can make a round trip to Betterton and back, including the side trips into Lloyd and Turner Creek for a total length of 25 miles. Or you can leave a shuttle vehicle by Betterton's swimming beach and create a one-way journey.

Put-in Site: The Turner Creek Park's boat landing is adjacent to the Sassafras River Natural Resource Management Area. There is no fee for launching or parking without a trailer. There are bathrooms and ample parking. Kayaks have their own launch site on a gravel beach, to the right, and opposite the powerboat ramp.

Driving Directions: Use MD 213, which can be accessed from US 301 from the South/Chesapeake Bay Bridge or from I-95 to the north at the head of the bay. If coming from the Chesapeake Bay Bridge, continue straight on US 301 when US 50/301 split. Exit onto 213 North toward Chestertown. Follow through Chestertown and continue on MD 213 for about 10 miles. Take a left onto Kennedyville Road. When it intersects with MD 298, cross straight over onto Turner Creek Road and follow until it ends at the landing. If you miss Kennedyville Road (which happens frequently), take a hard left on MD 298 South by Vonnie's

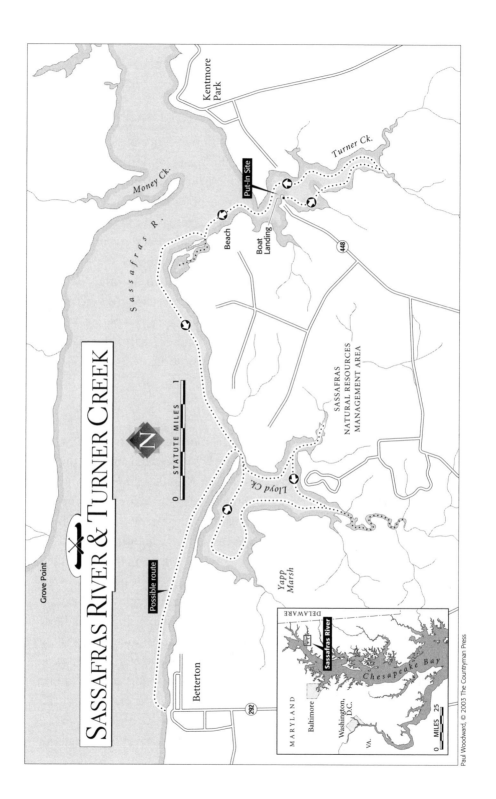

SASSAFRAS RIVER & TURNER CREEK

Grove Point

Money Ck.

Sassafras R.

Kentmore Park

Put-In Site

Turner Ck.

Beach

Boat Landing

448

SASSAFRAS NATURAL RESOURCES MANAGEMENT AREA

Lloyd Ck.

Yapp Marsh

N

STATUTE MILES

0   1

Possible route

Betterton

292

MARYLAND

DELAWARE

Sassafras River

Baltimore

Chesapeake Bay

Washington, D.C.

VA.

0   MILES   25

Paul Woodward, © 2003 The Countryman Press

Store and then take a right onto Turner Creek in about 1 ½ miles.

THE LOWER REACHES of the Sassafras have everything that I look for in a kayak trip. This waterway is a combination of peaceful side creeks for poke boating and the wide waters of the open river for stretching your paddling muscles. The boat landing in Turner Creek provides access to a leafy green refuge with a magical grove of lotus unlike anywhere else on the bay. On sunny weekends, the wakes from powerboats in the distant channel create oceanlike swells as they glide over the gently sloping and shallow shoreline of the wide river, making the cliff-side paddling experience more like a trip off the coast of Baja than any other place on the eastern shore of Maryland. When the sun is hot, the river's jellyfish-free, clear, fresh water and firm sand bottom, creates a perfect swimming environment. While this is hardly a wilderness trip, the Sassafras ranks high on my list of favorite paddling locations.

Paddling Notes

I prefer to head up Turner Creek in the morning to start my day with some peaceful and meditative paddling before I go out and play on the Sassafras. From the landing, the river is across and to the left, so hug the right-hand (southwestern) shoreline to head upstream on Turner. If you scan the mid–tree line as you paddle, it is rare not to spot a bald eagle roosted in the midst of the greenery. Once you turn the first bend and enter into a broad and shallow cove, you will begin to enter a thick stand of American lotus. Do not skirt the edges or be otherwise wary of these beautiful and mammoth plants—point your kayak toward the heart of the array and paddle forth. The lotus has a single broad leaf measuring up to 2 feet across and a single 5 to 10 inch large yellow blossom in the center, and is the only lotus native to North America. A stiff stem that is rooted into the river bottom supports it, and unlike spatterdock the stem can bear the full weight of the plant out of the water. At the highest tides you can paddle over the top the broad leaves, scaring off the turtles and frogs that perch upon them. However, the pads are generally held above the water and at low tide you can paddle completely under them. You should not pass up this strange and unique experience. All you will see of your paddling companions are their paddle blades rhythmically dipping and rising above the leaves and flowers. The lotus is even thicker on the other side of the small peninsula that divides the cove. An inlet has formed over the years, transforming the peninsula into an island and the passage is navigable at all but the lowest of tides. By taking this shortcut you are able to extend your adventure amongst the lotus.

When you emerge from the lotus forest, you should continue to bear right along the shore. Follow the creek's fork to the right and then hug the left (southern) side of this fork to paddle the clearwater passage past a dense mat of spatterdock and lotus. You may have to duck under some of the low hanging branches of the forest to your left, but push through to the deep pool of water beyond the lilies. Slip through the narrow inlet and you are transported into a secret paradise that few people ever see. The marsh is spectacularly diverse and lush, and muskrat and beaver can often be spotted swimming in its sheltered waters. The passage only lasts ¼ mile before your progress is stopped by a beaver dam, however this little stretch of water is a worthy destination and journey in and of itself.

After heading back down Turner, be alert when you near the mouth. The traffic at the entrance can be voluminous, so you need to shake the peaceful daze that was induced by the upstream waters. The boat channel follows the opposite (western) side of the mouth, so paddle directly across the opening, with a slight veer to the right, to bring you out into the open waters of the Sassafras. For the next ½ mile there is a beautiful stretch of beach that is one of my favorite lunch or snack spots in Maryland. There can be some breaking waves here from the powerboat wakes, so be alert when landing and wait for a lull if you are unsure of your surfing ability. A half mile from Turner Creek, the beach is interrupted by an inlet to a shallow cove, usually too shallow for any decent exploring. The tidal current is dramatically compressed in this inlet. When it is strongly ebbing, it will stack up the incoming swells into a long rolling break that is ideal for kayak surfing. There are commonly families picnicking here, with their powerboats beached or anchored out.

Once you round the point by the inlet, the Sassafras's shore dips back to the south and the depth is even shallower, giving you a huge area all to yourself. The bottom here is hard sand, but the beaches are generally not as good, composed mostly of hard, slick clay. However, there are still some good break spots hidden along the creases of the ancient cliffs. In about 2 miles you will come upon the narrow entrance that leads into the wide cove of Lloyd Creek. The depth here ranges from 3 to 0 feet, so try to time your explorations for high tide. The main stem of the Creek lies directly south of the entrance, and is delightful in its multiple meanders between forested and marsh-lined banks. The right side (western) slough into Yapp marsh and the left (eastern) branch into the woods are also beautiful, containing plenty of wading birds hunting their shallows.

After playing in Lloyd Creek, I usually head the 2½ miles back to Turner Creek. However, you can continue to the left and paddle another 2 miles west to the little town of Betterton, which is near the mouth of the Sassafras, facing north toward Aberdeen Proving Grounds across the bay. I wasted away many a wonderful day in college on this beach, listening to the booming detonation of bombs and cannons. You could leave a shuttle vehicle here, but why do this when you have a fun river like the Sassafras waiting for your return trip upstream?

17. *Chestertown/Chester River and Morgan Creek*

> **Length:** *Chestertown/Chester River:* From the put-in spot to Chestertown and back is 7 miles. *Morgan Creek:* From the put-in up Morgan Creek to its headwater and back is about 8 miles. Put them together and you can do a 15-mile trip.
>
> **Put-in Site:** Morgan Creek just northeast of Chestertown for both trips.
>
> **Driving Directions:** From Annapolis, take US 50 east across the Chesapeake Bay Bridge. Take US 301 north at the US 50/301 split. Take a right exit onto MD 213 north toward Chestertown. Follow MD 213 into Chestertown. Shortly after passing Wash-

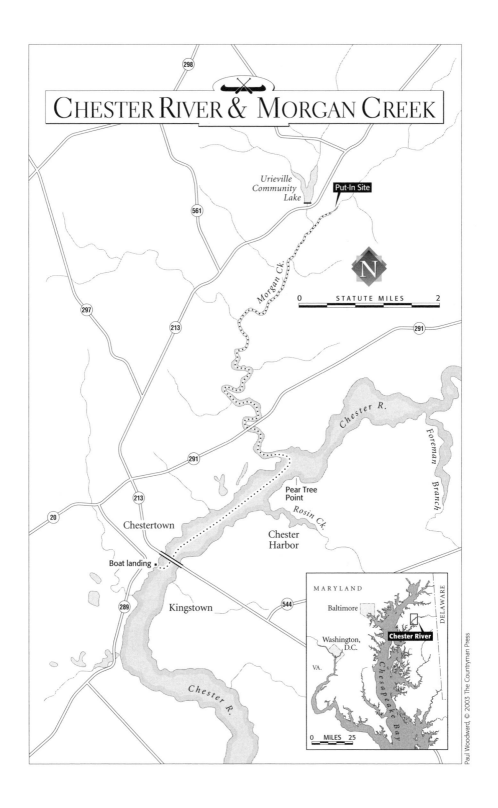

CHESTER RIVER & MORGAN CREEK

298

561

Urieville
Community
Lake

Put-In Site

Morgan Ck.

297

213

N

0   STATUTE MILES   2

291

Chester R.

Foreman Branch

291

Pear Tree
Point

213

Rosin Ck.

20

Chestertown

Chester
Harbor

Boat landing

289

Kingstown

544

MARYLAND

Baltimore

DELAWARE

Chester River

Washington,
D.C.

VA.

Chesapeake Bay

0   MILES   25

Chester R.

Paul Woodward, © 2003 The Countryman Press

ington College you will intersect with MD 291 (shopping center at other side of intersection). Take a right onto MD 291 and follow it out of town. Immediately after crossing a blue steel bridge you will see a dirt road loop and the put-in spot on your left—park off the dirt road on the grass.

CHESTERTOWN was a port of entry during colonial times and was founded in 1706. A stroll down just about any street will give you a taste of history as you pass beautiful, fully restored old houses from the 18th century. There are all types of shops and restaurants and handsome streets to wander. Chestertown is the home of Washington College, the 10th oldest liberal arts college in the country and where George Washington sat on the board. You can paddle from Morgan Creek to Chester River to Chestertown and return, or just paddle up Morgan Creek and return.

Paddling Notes

From the put-in to Chestertown: This put-in is a little rustic. Although it is close to the road and not far from town, it is undeveloped and suitable for small, human-powered craft. Few powerboats frequent this area. The bank can be a little blunt and slippery. Try putting your kayak in the water completely before entering and use your paddle as a brace. You may have to get your feet wet on this one. From the put-in spot on Morgan Creek, head left (east) for just over a mile where Morgan Creek dumps into the Chester. At the confluence of Morgan Creek and the Chester River head right (south). Follow the river 2½ miles to Chestertown.

During low tide there are many places to take a break along the way; it is just the opposite during high tide. This stretch of Morgan Creek offers few places to exit your kayak. A keen search, however, will reveal some nice spots if you are willing to get your feet wet and duck under some trees at the water's edge. You may also find some small beaches at low tide.

Along the bank of the Chester River, as you head to town, there are many houses and a good bit of the bank is bulkheaded, which makes landing tough or impossible during high tide, but possible during low tide. Some areas near the bulkheads have small beaches at low tide. Be prepared to paddle from the put-in spot to Chestertown without a chance to exit onto dry land.

Along the way you are likely to notice red-winged blackbirds, kingfishers, signs of muskrat habitat, and some freshwater fish swirling around your kayak. If you are lucky, you may even see a bald eagle. Paddle close to the edges of Morgan Creek in the spring. Your kayak will cause a ruckus as schools of small, spawning fish (usually mummichogs; see page 112) swim for cover. You are a huge great blue heron to them, or maybe some kind of freaky top- water fish. These guys go crazy trying to get away from you, often bouncing across the surface as a frog would in very shallow water.

Once on the Chester, on the bank to your right, little habitat is left for small fish. You still may see a great blue heron fishing or perhaps a northern brown water snake swimming by. But, for the most part, as mentioned above, the bank is bulk-headed along the way to town.

No need to lose heart, there are other wonders to absorb. Keep an eye out for some of the most beautiful sailboats around; perhaps a nice-sized yacht or a skipjack, one of the original ships used to dredge oysters during the 1800s and early 1900s and unique to the Chesapeake Bay.

Keep paddling down the Chester and shortly after you pass under the MD 213 bridge you will come to the High Street public dock area at the edge of Chestertown on your right. Paddle a little further and take out at a parking lot for a marina/restaurant because it is a difficult take-out at the dock due to a man-made stone bank. Be sure to ask for permission to keep your kayak on the restaurant property.

From here you can walk around and get a feel for Chestertown. Travel up High Street; grab some lunch from one of the many restaurants in town. A chocolate shake or fountain soda from Durding's Drugstore, with an original old-fashioned ice cream parlor, is your reward for paddling to town. After a nice stroll through town you can continue further downstream on the Chester and take in the rest of the Chestertown waterfront, or return to Morgan Creek. You could also paddle past Morgan Creek and up the Chester a little farther. You will experience a more natural environment beyond Morgan Creek.

From the put-in up Morgan Creek and back: If you desire a pristine and serene paddle with the likelihood of avoiding boat traffic, paddle up Morgan Creek instead of to Chestertown. Paddle right from the put-in spot. Morgan Creek meanders for miles with undisturbed shoreline and freshwater-tidal marshlands. You will also experience forested wetlands as well as upland forest. Notice the change in plant life as elevation rises.

This paddle is absolutely gorgeous. If you have a seine net you can find a place to drag it and see what you find. The water is often silted and quite turbid, making visibility difficult. But, there are many critters and fish below you. While leading a kayak trip a few years ago my group and I came upon a husband and wife fishing from the bank. When asked what they were catching the husband pulled up a 13-pound snapping turtle. Incredible! It was prehistoric looking with knobby ridges on its shell and a razor sharp beak. These folks went on to explain how they caught turtles there regularly for meat and soup and described how to dress a turtle and different ways to cook them. Great story and a quick peek into the life of some locals.

I could go on and on about what you will possibly see while paddling up Morgan Creek. Just know the potential is there to witness a great variety of plant, reptile, fish, and bird life as well as muskrat, fox, and nutria.

Lunch spots are challenging to find. But, if you get up close to a forested bank you will notice great places for lunch just up the shore. A boat landing exists 2½ miles or so upstream on the left where you can stop. Try to paddle all the way to the headwaters. Enjoy the changes as you go.

Note of caution: Beware of boat traffic on both of these trips. On the Chester River keep to the right and hug the shore as you head to town. Avoid crossing the river. On Morgan Creek, pick a side and stick with it. Cross with caution if necessary. There is very little boat traffic on Morgan Creek, but an occasional angler may speed in and out.

18. *Eastern Neck Island National Wildlife Refuge*

Length: Circumnavigation: 9 miles minimum. You can also do out and back trips as long or as short as you desire.

Put-in Site: Bogles Wharf

Driving Directions: From Annapolis, take US 50/301 across the Chesapeake Bay Bridge, Stay on US 301. When US 301 and US 50 split, exit onto MD 213 north. Follow MD 213 through Chestertown. Take a left onto MD 20 toward Rock Hall (at an intersection). In Rock Hall, take a left on MD 445 (Eastern Neck Island Rd.). Once on the island, take a left on Bogles Warf Road and follow to the parking lot at Bogles Wharf on Durdin Creek. Maps are usually available as you enter the park.

EASTERN NECK ISLAND NATIONAL WILDLIFE REFUGE (ENNWR) is a spit of land disconnected from the mainland by just a few yards, which makes it easy to access. The refuge, established in 1962, contains 2,285 acres. During the winter Eastern Neck is considered a major feeding and resting area for migratory waterfowl. Many birds overwinter here as well. The endangered Delmarva fox squirrel resides and is protected here and also at the Blackwater National Wildlife Refuge (page 156).

The beauty of this paddle is that one can experience the feel of paddling on the open Chesapeake while being protected from boat traffic. The protected marsh environment housed in the coves and shoreline of the eastern side of the refuge offers a completely different paddling experience.

According to the Kent Count Government web site "the ENNWR includes 1,000 acres of brackish marsh, 600 acres of cropland, 500 acres of forest, 100 acres of grassland and 40 acres of open water impoundments. It is home to three threatened and/or endangered species of birds; mammals at the refuge include white-tailed deer, beaver, red fox, raccoons, muskrat, opossum, woodchuck, eastern gray squirrel and, as mentioned above, the endangered Delmarva fox squirrel." Used as a foraging ground by Native Americans 10 thousand years ago, this island refuge has a very interesting and extensive history. Check out:

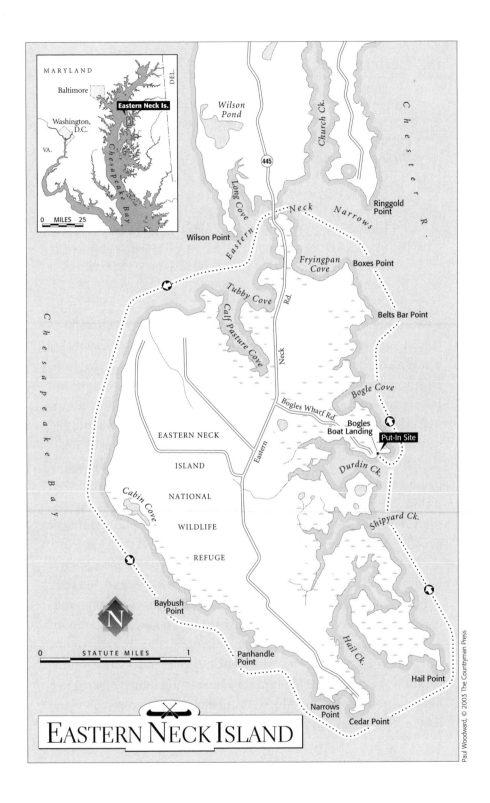

MARYLAND

Baltimore

Washington, D.C.

VA.

DEL.

Chesapeake Bay

Eastern Neck Is.

0   MILES   25

Wilson Pond

Church Ck.

445

Chester R.

Neck Narrows

Ringgold Point

Long Cove

Wilson Point

Eastern

Fryingpan Cove

Boxes Point

Tubby Cove

Neck Rd.

Belts Bar Point

Calf pasture Cove

Neck

Bogle Cove

Bogles Wharf Rd.

Bogles Boat Landing

Put-In Site

EASTERN NECK

Eastern

Durdin Ck.

ISLAND

Shipyard Ck.

Cabin Cove

NATIONAL

WILDLIFE

REFUGE

N

Baybush Point

Hail Ck.

0   STATUTE MILES   1

Panhandle Point

Narrows Point

Cedar Point

Hail Point

EASTERN NECK ISLAND

www.kentcounty.com/gov/parkrec/parks/eneck.htm for an excellent and brief explanation (online map available here as well).

Paddling Notes

Circumnavigate Eastern Neck Island: There is a good-sized parking lot at this landing. Be sure to get your kayak and gear ready off to the side of the boat landing so you do not block others from putting in. Many local folks who crab and fish the area use the landing. Paddling around Eastern Neck Island is pretty straightforward. The trip is just 9 miles if you do not duck into the smaller coves, which is highly recommended. Start at Bogles Wharf and, turning left, paddle north to circumnavigate the island. It is best to paddle the open water early in the day due to the possibility of afternoon squalls and prevailing southern winds in the warmer months. There is better protection on the eastern side, and the wind will most likely be at your back as you return.

You will exit Durdin Creek, onto the Chester River, pass Bogle Cove, and curve northwest past Fryingpan Cove to Eastern Neck Narrows. Be alert for small boat traffic here and quicker tidal current because the water is squeezed between the island and the mainland as it passes under the bridge connecting the two. Occasionally, boats will motor through this narrow channel leaving little room for the kayaker. Kayakers can also get stuck on the bridge pilings which will probably cause a capsize. Also, watch for folks fishing from the bridge. Their lines hang down directly into the channel and it is easy to get tangled and generally frustrate the anglers (not to mention experiencing the thrill of being a fish caught on a hook). Communicate with the fishermen/women if your way is blocked.

If you are planning a short out and back paddle, consider paddling to the shore on the right after passing under the bridge and follow it out to the Chesapeake. Round the point and head north. There are some very nice beaches here on the mainland.

Hug the shoreline to the left as much as possible after passing through the bridge. This will protect you from boat traffic and get you out of moving water as soon as possible. Keep paddling to Tubby Cove or Calf Pasture Cove. Both areas have some beach and are good places to take a break. The water surrounding this area is very shallow. Often locals are out wading and looking for crabs, and this is a great place to wade and swim on a hot day.

Once you are past Calf Pasture Cove you will experience paddling the open bay. Look northwest and you may be able to spot Baltimore on a clear day. Usually this stretch is a serene and enjoyable paddle. Along the way you can dip between some stone breakwaters and the island for an extra smooth paddling experience. Be sure to take a break somewhere along the bay side of Eastern Neck Island. You will be amazed at the different flotsam strewn along the shore (feel free to take some trash back with you to dispose of properly).

Bail out option: If you get caught in some serious weather on this side of Eastern Neck Island, you can bail out at Ingleside Recreation Area (see map) and you only have to paddle ⅓ of the island. From here you can hike back to your car at Bogles Wharf or seek help at the ranger station.

Keep your eye open for Cabin Cove, a small lake on this side of the island that you may be able to access. It is about halfway down as you travel south, but somewhat hidden. Access is via a small channel and may not be noticeable if you are outside the riprap. After Cabin Cove your journey begins to veer east, although you are still traveling to the south of the island. There are some excellent beaches on the southern end for picnicking, beachcombing and swimming. If the wind is right you can practice a little surfing and beach landing. From here you should be able to spot the Kent Island Narrows area, south across the Chester. Don't try to cross over to it—powerboat traffic rules this area.

Believe it or not, you have been paddling in the Chester River, for the most part, since Cabin Cove. As you round Cedar Point, the southernmost tip of Eastern Neck Island, you begin a northward journey up the Chester and back to Bogles Wharf. Along the way the environment and topography return to that of a tidal, brackish marsh. Be sure to explore Hail Creek just past Cedar Point for a true wetlands experience. If you have the time and energy take pleasure in paddling the nooks and crannies on this side of the island. There are small coves and slues lined with cordgrass, salt meadow hay and marsh elder with a backdrop of towering pines. You can escape the wind and paddle in total silence or drift for a while observing whatever wildlife may be around. Have you ever tried dozing while drifting in your kayak on a warm sunny day? Try it. Just make sure you stay out of harm's way.

As you continue north past Hail Point you will pass Shipyard Creek, (another great place to explore) and then finally reach Durdin Creek and Bogles Wharf. For more paddling, you can continue north up the Chester River. For a shorter trip head out in either direction from Durdin Creek depending on the environment you want to paddle.

For more information on the Eastern Neck National Wildlife Refuge go to the U.S. Fish and Wildlife Service web page: http://easternneck.fws.gov/. Or call the park office: 410-639-7056.

19. *Prospect Bay West Near Kent Island Narrows*

Length: Approximately 9 miles from Goodhands Creek landing to Parsons Island and back. Add mileage for exploring coves and creeks and circumnavigating Parsons Island (circumnavigation of Parsons Island is just a little more than 2 miles).

Put-in Site: Goodhands Creek boat landing.

Note: Each car in your party will need a day permit from Queen Anne's County. The cost is $5 (2002). Obtain permits at Angler's Sport Center: 1456 Whitehall Road, Annapolis, MD, 410-757-3442 or Queen Anne's County Tourism Office: 425 Piney Narrows Road, Chester, MD, 410-604-2100. Year permits are available as well.)

Driving Directions: From the Chesapeake Bay Bridge head East on US 50 to MD 552 south (Exit 39 B). Take MD 552 approximately ¾ mile and turn left onto Goodhands Creek Road. Follow to the boat landing.

Alternate shuttle put-in: Take US 50 East across the Bay Bridge and exit at MD 8, the first exit on US 50. Follow MD 8 south to Great Neck Road and turn left to Warehouse Creek boat landing. There will be a small gravel and dirt parking area on the

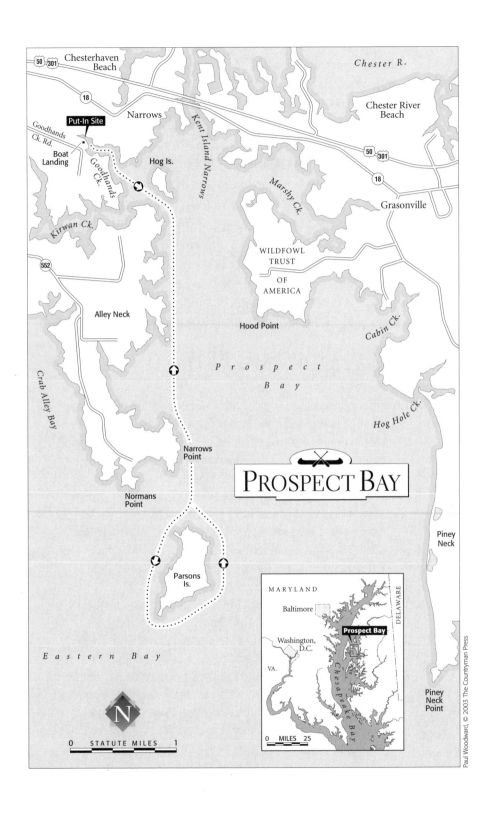

Chesterhaven
Beach

50 301

18

Narrows

Put-In Site

Goodhands
Ck. Rd.

Boat
Landing

Goodhands Ck.

Hog Is.

Kent Island Narrows

Chester R.

Chester River
Beach

50 301

18

Grasonville

Marshy Ck.

WILDFOWL
TRUST
OF
AMERICA

Kirwan Ck.

552

Alley Neck

Crab Alley Bay

Hood Point

Cabin Ck.

Prospect
Bay

Hog Hole Ck.

Narrows
Point

Normans
Point

Parsons
Is.

Eastern Bay

PROSPECT BAY

Piney
Neck

Piney
Neck
Point

N

0   STATUTE MILES   1

MARYLAND

Baltimore

Washington,
D.C.

VA.

DELAWARE

Prospect Bay

Chesapeake Bay

0   MILES   25

Paul Woodward, © 2003 The Countryman Press

right. The landing is accessible to small boats only (permit required).

KENT ISLAND NARROWS is a skinny channel of water squeezed between Kent Island (on its west) and the rest of the eastern shore. This particular waterway is not very friendly for kayakers, but Prospect Bay just south of the narrows is mighty hospitable. One of the great things about this trip is its proximity to the Baltimore, Washington, D.C., and Annapolis area. It offers great paddling on the eastern shore and is a shorter drive than many of the other trips described in this guide. Another highlight is its relatively undeveloped shoreline.

Paddling Notes

This area is a tidal brackish environment except perhaps at the extreme reaches of the tops of the creeks. Along the way you will enjoy saltwater marshland, some beautiful but small sandy beaches, and forests of pine. Be sure to take a chance and get out on the marsh to feel how the roots hold everything together.

From the boat landing head right (southeast) to the mouth of Goodhands Creek and out to Prospect Bay. At the mouth of Goodhands Creek will be Hog Island. You may notice a nest of mute swans, whose eggs are approximately 3 inches in diameter (although beautiful, mute swans are not native to the Chesapeake and, due to their voracious appetite for underwater grasses, are detrimental to the stability of water quality and wildlife habitat). The water on the east side of Hog Island is nice and deep. Take a break and watch for feeding fish. To avoid boat traffic, this is about as far east from the shore you should travel. Heading south along the western side of Prospect Bay you will pass Kirwan Creek, which is fun to explore since there is very little development. It is about a 1-mile paddle to the top of the creek.

Continuing south to Narrows Point you will pass tidal brackish water wetlands, some pine forests, and several small beaches where you can take a break—good places to do some beachcombing or hang out in the sun. The last time I paddled here I found the tiny shell of a horse-

Taking a break on Prospect Bay

shoe crab that had molted, and even came across a pair of mating horseshoe crabs (usually at the end of May into June). There is a large cove a couple of miles into your paddle just north of Narrows Point. Powerboats and personal watercraft are known to fly through this area so I suggest keeping to the shore, especially on weekends. If all is safe you can cross from the southern part of Narrows Point or maybe a little further south from Normans Point to Parsons Island. The distance is a little shorter from the southern tip of Narrows Point.

Parsons Island has some sandy and rocky beaches where you can break for lunch. Please be aware that the island is private property. Do your best to stay below the high-tidewater line and keep to the beach area. Paddling around the island is nice because it protects you from powerboaters and offers you the feeling of open water paddling. Mute swans have been spotted here as well.

If you are feeling adventurous and have a good deal of energy, there is plenty more paddling to be found. South of Parsons Island is Eastern Bay, very exposed water with no place to hide in case of a storm or boat traffic. It is best to avoid this area. If you plan to continue south, cross back to Narrows Point and hug the shore. Head southwest around Narrows Point into Crab Alley Bay and Creek. For those looking to push it, continue on around Turkey Point and head up Cox Creek to Warehouse Creek or Thompson Creek.

An alternative to a round-trip launching from Goodhands Creek is to do a shuttle. You can leave a car at the small boat landing on Warehouse Creek off Great Neck Road (see directions above), and a car at the landing for Goodhands Creek. This way you can launch from either place and paddle one way. This is at least a 15-mile trip depending on how much you hug the shore.

Look at a good map. Continuing from Parsons Island into Crab Alley you may want to stop at Johnson Island and Little Island at the mouth of Crab Alley Creek. These two islands are safer and easier to get to since they are less exposed to boat traffic than Bodkin and Long Marsh Island off Turkey Point.

Once past Turkey Point head north up Cox Creek. Find a narrow spot and cross over to head northwest up Warehouse Creek. Your take-out will be on the right almost all the way up the creek. This is a beautiful paddle all the way with a good mixture of undisturbed shoreline and some interesting and huge houses.

Unpacking the kayak after a great day on Warehouse Creek

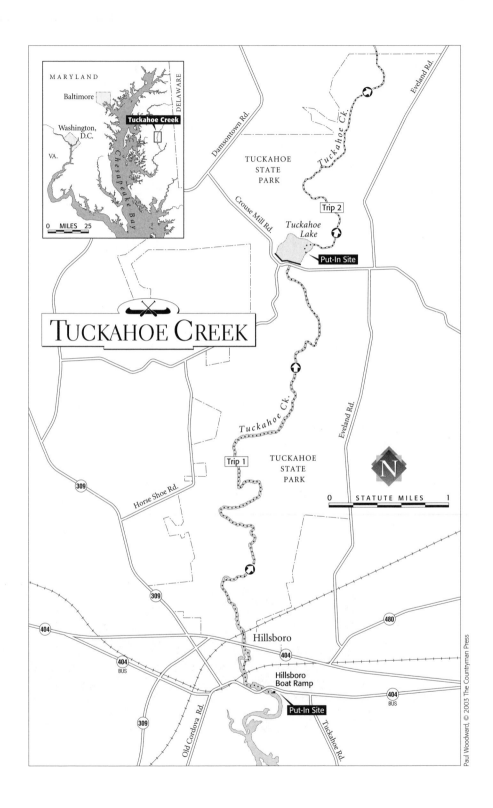

MARYLAND

Baltimore

Washington, D.C.

VA.

DELAWARE

Tuckahoe Creek

Chesapeake Bay

0 MILES 25

Damsontown Rd.

Eveland Rd.

Tuckahoe Ck.

TUCKAHOE STATE PARK

Crouse Mill Rd.

Trip 2

Tuckahoe Lake

Put-In Site

TUCKAHOE CREEK

Tuckahoe Ck.

Eveland Rd.

Trip 1

TUCKAHOE STATE PARK

N

0 STATUTE MILES 1

309

Horse Shoe Rd.

309

480

404

404 BUS

Hillsboro

404

Hillsboro Boat Ramp

404 BUS

309

Old Cordova Rd.

Put-In Site

Tuckahoe Rd.

20. *Tuckahoe Creek, Upper Section: Tributary of the Choptank River*

Length: Hillsboro Bridge to Crouse Mill Road: approximately 10 miles (round trip) depending on water level. Tuckahoe Lake to as far as possible upstream (Mason Branch Trail): approximately 6 miles (round trip) depending on water level.

Put-in Site: *Trip 1:* Hillsboro Bridge on Talbot Avenue. *Trip 2:* Lake at Tuckahoe Creek State Park.

Driving Directions: *Trip 1:* From the Chesapeake Bay Bridge follow US 50/301 over the Chesapeake Bay Bridge. Take US 50 east to MD 404 and go left toward Hillsboro and Denton. As you approach Queen Anne, go right on MD 309 toward Queen Anne (there will be a Shell Station on your right and a Royal Crown across MD 309 on your right). This is the last place to use the bathroom and get supplies. On MD 309 you will soon come to a stop sign. Go straight onto MD 303. On your left you will see Queen Anne Grain Company and some huge silos. Go to the next stop sign and turn left onto Talbot Ave. (T intersection). You are less than a ½ mile from the boat landing. Follow Talbot Ave. and cross the Tuckahoe. The boat landing/put-in spot will be the first right after you cross the Tuckahoe. Pull in and park and please make sure not to block the boat landing.

This put-in has a small boat landing and limited parking. However, traffic is light and we have never had trouble parking. Use the shore so larger craft have access to the landing.

Trip 2: Above Tuckahoe Creek State Park put-in. Take US 50 across the Chesapeake Bay Bridge and continue on 50. Take a left on MD 404 (at a traffic light). At second traffic light take a left on MD 480. Take the next left onto Eveland Road. Follow this into the park. Go to a T-intersection and turn left, toward the fishing area. Follow this road around to the boat landing.

Side Trip: Adkins Arboretum: "a 400-acre preserve operated by a private, nonprofit agency within the park boundaries." Take a stroll on their 3½ mile trail. www.adkinsarboretum.org.

THE FIRST TIME I drove across this creek it pulled me to paddle it. The image of this lush tunnel of greenery surrounding sparkling water stayed with me for months. I did not even know the name of the place, but finally got back and made the trip. It is amazing to have such a beautiful and unspoiled waterway such a short distance from Annapolis. Once you paddle here you will most likely want to return again and again. The name Tuckahoe may have several origins: sassafras, a root Native Americans used to make a form of bread; *Tuckas,* a rounded root used for food; or *Tuckahoe,* a fungus pressed together at the base and roots.

I will describe two paddling trips for Tuckahoe Creek—*Trip 1:* Hillsboro Bridge to Crouse Mill Road (Dam); *Trip 2:* Tuckahoe Creek State Park as far as possible upstream.

Trip 1: Hillsboro Bridge to Crouse Mill Road

This section of the Tuckahoe is a tidal freshwater environment most of the way. It eventually turns nontidal. Try to time your paddle to go with the flood tide on the way upstream in order to paddle as far as possible. The freshwater environment (and the protection of undeveloped creek bank) allows for a greater variety of plant and animal species than a brackish water environment.

From the put-in, paddle right (north). For the first ½ mile or so you will pass some businesses and old canneries on the west side and go under four bridges. After the third bridge the creek is buffered by ½ to more than 1 mile on each side by Tuckahoe State Park. From here up to the dam (and beyond) there is no development, only a farm and the state park. The shoreline is shrouded in overhanging greenery and several small streams flow into the Tuckahoe from all directions. For the most part the floor of this stretch of Tuckahoe Creek is sandy and makes for easy wading and swimming. Many shallow areas allow one to exit the kayak and relax on a gravelly sand bar. However, mud does exist. Break spots along the shore will require getting your feet muddy. Many take-out spots exist, but test the area with your paddle— you could easily sink to your thighs in Tuckahoe detritus.

Other features include high banks, islands, forested wetlands, and a great deal of wildlife. On our paddles we have observed: mud, musk,

Mike Savario

Launching at Lake Tuckahoe to paddle the upper section

eastern painted, and redbelly turtles (see page 138), northern brown water snakes, a variety of fish (including American shad), muskrat, beaver, Canadian geese, osprey (see page 22) great blue heron (see page 161), kingfisher, bald eagle (see page 33), pileated woodpecker, red-tailed hawk, red-winged blackbird and a variety of other small birds. Of all these the eastern painted and redbelly turtles are the easiest to spot on warm days.

The tide, freshwater flow, and fallen trees determine the distance one can navigate by kayak. The staff from the state park scouts the creek in the spring to clear a path for paddlers and do their best to keep the environment natural. Sometimes there is just enough room in a cut out tree for a kayak to pass. You may be required to drag your kayak across shallow areas or blown down trees. The rewards are worth the trouble, but beware of poison ivy. It is a bumper crop in Maryland and often grows on fallen trees that cross the water.

If you want to paddle more, on your return, pass the boat landing and continue downstream. You can paddle for miles. A half-mile or so

Mike Savario

Admiring the beauty as the Tuckahoe narrows

past the landing Tuckahoe Creek widens and the environment changes from one of overhanging greenery to open expanses of freshwater marsh backed by forest. Along the way you will find a nice beach or two. This area is just as beautiful as upstream, but quite different. The water is brownish due to a bottom of silt and runoff rather than sand and gravel. There is the possibility of strong winds due to greater fetch, and the current can flow faster, especially the ebb flow. Also beware of the occasional powerboat. A possible trip would be to put in at Hillsboro and take out at Covey's Landing a distance of 5½ miles on the western shore of the Tuckahoe. Or go another 5 miles to New Bridge Landing, also on the western side. Or, paddle to the Choptank and cross it to take out at Ganeys Wharf a little more than 3 miles from New Bridge Landing. You would need to shuttle. (Total mileage from Hillsboro to Ganeys Wharf: approximately 14 miles or more depending on how tightly you hug the shores.) You will pass the birthplace of Frederick Douglass (1817), who escaped from slavery in the early 1800s, just south of Mill Creek on the western side of Tuckahoe Creek. There exist many smaller creeks to explore on the way. Keep in mind that exploring these creeks will add more mileage to your journey.

Trip 2: Tuckahoe Lake and Upstream

TUCKAHOE CREEK STATE PARK boasts 3,800 total acres following the flow of the Tuckahoe, a 60-acre lake, 15 miles of trails for hiking, horseback riding and mountain biking and fishing. The put-in/boat landing is on Tuckahoe Lake, a perfect place to warm up and practice strokes or rescues. Powerboats are not allowed so serenity rules. From the landing paddle east and hug the shore and you will eventually merge with Tuckahoe Creek. It may be challenging to find the creek on your first attempt. This paddle will bring you through forested wetlands, high banks, and a shroud of greenery in the spring and summer months. In areas the water is crystal clear allowing you to see the American shad and other fish species. Pileated woodpeckers live here along with bald eagles, osprey, blue herons, kingfishers and smaller birds. The water is always cool and there are great places to break and take a swim.

21. Wye Island Natural Resource Management Area

> **Length:** You can paddle as short or as long a distance as you like. Circumnavigation is 14 miles minimum, but you can go out and back rather than circumnavigate.

Turtles

Many species of turtles exist in the Chesapeake watershed. Sometimes you have to look hard to spot one and other times they are everywhere; it depends on where you are paddling. Keep an eye out for these: the eastern painted, redbelly, musk, mud, and terrapin turtles. Brief descriptions of each follow.

Eastern painted turtles, *Chrysemys picta picta,* can be seen sunning themselves on logs and other substrate protruding from the water. From a distance you may be able to spot one by looking for something shiny since its shell may still be wet and reflecting light. The carapace is trimmed in red and the legs are marked in red. Neck stripes are red as well and turn to yellow on the side of the head and chin. With binoculars you can see their colorful eyes. Also look for two yellow spots behind each eye. As you get closer the turtles will plop into the water. Feeds on a variety of prey including mollusks, insects, crustaceans, and plants.

Redbelly turtle, *Pseudemys rubriventris rubriventris,* is the largest basking turtle of fresh and brackish marshes. The carapace is black with red markings and the plastron is red. Light lines on the top of the head may meet a line that passes through the eye and continue on to form an arrow at the snout. When these guys hit the water you know it. They can get up to almost 16 inches in length. The redbelly is an omnivore and feeds on crayfish, insect larvae, snails, and vegetation.

Musk turtle, *Sternotherus odoratus,* or stinkpot, is a small turtle often seen crawling around on the bottom just below the surface in shallow water. It is brown and small with two light stripes on its head. Stinkpot is its nickname because it gives off scent when stressed, much like a black rat snake or fox. Usually feeds on the bottom at night for mollusks, crayfish, aquatic insects, and carrion.

Eastern mud turtle, *Kinosternon subrubrum subrubrum,* is also found in shallow areas and is the only mud turtle in the Chesapeake region. The back of the shell is yellowish brown to black and the belly is yellowish with two hinges. The mud turtle is also small, 3 to 4 inches, and looks similar to the musk turtle. It feeds on aquatic insects, crustaceans, carrion, and may look for food on land.

Northern diamondback terrapin, *Malaclemys terrapin,* is an elusive little critter. I have seen very few terrapin on land or basking in the sun. This is the only turtle of saltwater marshes. You can spot their noses poking through the surface. They often just look like the tip of a stick poking out 1 to 3 inches above the water. When the stick disappears you know you spotted one. On the upper scute of the carapace are diamond shaped rings. The carapace is a dull gray. These turtles, once considered a delicacy, were almost over-harvested into extinction in the 1920s. Terrapins are still protected with limited trapping allowed. Females can reach 9 inches and males up to 5½ inches. Terrapins feed on clams, worms, snails, crabs, carrion, and vegetation.

Other turtles that are abundant in the areas we describe in this guide, but are not seen as often when paddling, are the snapping turtle and box turtle. —*M.S.*

Put-in Site: Wye Landing and Bennett Point: At the time of this writing no launching from Wye Island is possible due to concerns about environmental impact. Both of these landings are across a small body of water from the island.

Driving Directions: *Wye Landing:* From the Chesapeake Bay Bridge take US 50 east to MD 662 and go right (south). Follow MD 662 through the small town of Wye Mills. Go right on Wye Landing Lane (looks like a residential road). Follow Wye Landing Lane until the end and park at the marina parking lot if possible. This is a popular landing, and most likely you will have to park along the road. In that case, you can drive to the boat landing, drop off your gear and park back on the road. *Wye Ferry Landing off Bennett Point Road:* From the Chesapeake Bay Bridge take US 50 east to exit 45 B. At the bottom of exit turn right. You are on Nesbitt Road. At MD 18 turn left (east) and follow to Bennett Point Road. Turn right. Take Bennett Point Road down to Wye Ferry Road and turn left. Follow to the boat landing.

Note: Each car in your party will need a day permit from Queen Anne's County. The cost is $5 (2002). Obtain permits at Angler's Sport Center: 1456 Whitehall Road, Annapolis, MD, 410-757-3442 or Queen Anne's County Tourism Office: 425 Piney Narrows Road, Chester, MD, 410-604-2100. Year permits are also available.

WYE ISLAND is a Natural Resource Management Area (NRMA) managed by the Maryland Department of Natural Resources, State Forest Service. The island is 2,800 acres. Maryland manages approximately 2,450 acres and the rest is privately owned. For more than 300 years Wye Island was privately owned and managed for agricultural use (the state obtained ownership in the 1970s).

In the 1770s Wye Island was a self-sufficient community whose main crop was wheat. In addition the island boasted its own vineyards, orchards, textile production, brickyard, and brewery. Even salt was produced from the Wye River. The island remained agricultural, being split up into parcels that changed ownership throughout the years until the 1970s, when it almost was developed into a modern community with

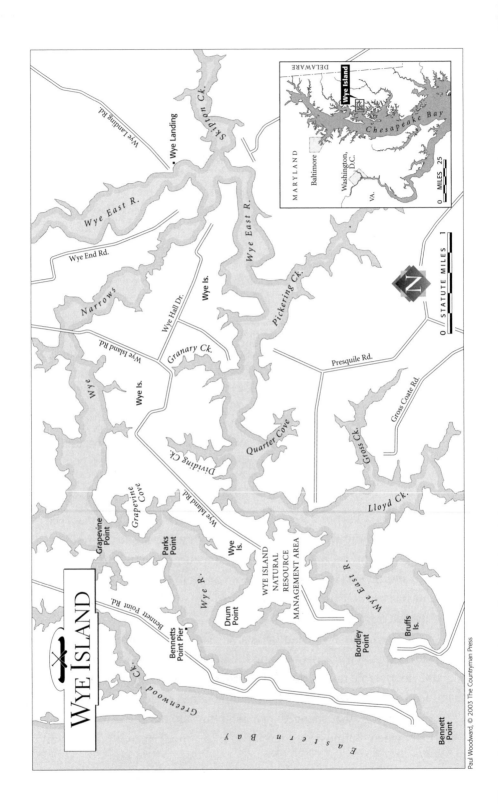

WYE ISLAND

Wye Landing Rd.
Wye Landing
Skipton Ck.
Wye East R.
Wye East R.
Wye End Rd.
Pickering Ck.
Narrows
Wye Hall Dr.
Wye Is.
Wye Island Rd.
Granary Ck.
Presquile Rd.
Wye Is.
Gross Coate Rd.
Wye Is.
Quarter Cove
Dividing Ck.
Gross Ck.
Grapevine Cove
Wye Island Rd.
Lloyd Ck.
Grapevine Point
Parks Point
Wye Is.
Wye R.
WYE ISLAND NATURAL RESOURCE MANAGEMENT AREA
Wye East R.
Bennett Point Rd.
Drum Point
Bennetts Point Pier
Bordley Point
Bruffs Is.
Greenwood Ck.
Eastern Bay
Bennett Point

STATUTE MILES 1
0

N

MARYLAND
DELAWARE
Baltimore
Washington, D.C.
VA.
Chesapeake Bay
Wye Island
MILES 25
0

its own stores, marinas, public utilities, and cluster housing. Fortunately, there was much opposition to this plan and the island was spared development.

In an effort to prevent further development attempts, and to preserve this unique resource, Maryland purchased the island and established the Wye Island NRMA. The Department of Natural Resources manages the island for agricultural and recreational use including agricultural research, hiking, paddling, biking, birding, group camping, volunteer projects, and hunting.

Paddling Notes

Paddling around Wye Island is a 14- to 15-mile trip if you take the shortest route and resist the urge to explore. The island possesses approximately 30 miles of shoreline. Thus, one could paddle many more miles by dipping in and out of its coves while circumnavigating. My favorite way to paddle Wye Island is to leave from Wye Landing, wander around its beautiful coves and perhaps a surrounding creek, and return to Wye Landing.

Much wildlife exists near these inlets. Keep an eye out for herons (see page 161), osprey, bald eagles, kingfishers, blue crabs, a variety of small fish, cownosed rays (see page 143), fox, turtles, and deer. There are some nice beaches at low tide and great places to swim. In addition, the island offers 6 miles of hiking trails as well as picnic areas.

Wye Island is surrounded by the Wye East River on the south and east side, and Wye River on the west/northwest side. There is also the Wye Narrows on the north side of the island. There is less large boat traffic in the narrows because of the low height of the bridge that provides auto access to Wye Island. Some beautiful creeks flow into these rivers: Pickering and Lloyd creeks on the south of the island, and Skipton Creek at the eastern end. All are worthy of exploration as following the Wye East River north away from the island.

One of the most beautiful places to paddle is Pickering Creek on the southeast side of the island. From Wye Landing head south out of the Wye East River and pass the eastern point of Wye Island to your right. You will pass Skipton Creek to your left. Follow Wye Island around and head west. It is just over 2 miles to the mouth of Pickering Creek, which flows from the southeast into the Wye East River. You have to cross the Wye East River from the island to get up Pickering. Use great caution and cross at the narrowest point. Keep to the shore along the way before you cross, as it is easy to drift into boat traffic channels.

Take some time and paddle up Pickering Creek. You will pass Pickering Creek Environmental Center on the right. You may be able to stop there for lunch (seek permission first). Continue paddling upstream and witness the beauty of a tidal brackish, and further up, freshwater creek.

The Wye Ferry Landing off Bennett Point Road puts you near the mouth of Wye River on the western side of the island. Again, this boat landing is not on Wye Island. Thus, you would need to make a short crossing to the island. This area is much more open than paddling from Wye Landing and can be subject to a good deal of boat traffic and some wind. From Wye Ferry Landing you can paddle around the southern tip of Wye Island called Bordley Point. This entire southern tip of the island is privately owned so please keep off unless you are experiencing an emergency.

Along this paddle you will get a glimpse of the open expanse of the Miles River and Eastern Bay, which the Wye River dumps before hitting the Chesapeake Bay. This is an interesting area to paddle because it offers a sense of open water experience and often there is some underwater activity near Bordley Point. Many times I have come across cownose rays (see next page) and other fish here. There is also some salt marsh that, because of erosion, has turned into little islands and also makes for fun paddling.

There are several places on the island to get out and take a break. Keep your eye open for a small beach or spit of land. The higher the tide the more difficult your quest will be. One of the best break spots is Dividing Creek on the southwestern side. As you paddle up the creek look for a small dock on the left side. Here you can land your kayak and take a break. There is great hiking from this spot and a pit toilet, compliments of a local Eagle Scout. This take-out area is very near a group

Cownose Rays *(Rhinoptera bonasus)*

There is nothing more exhilarating than calmly paddling along and suddenly spotting two shark-like looking fins speeding through the water near your kayak. Or having the water go crazy in a boiling fashion just below your craft. This can happen in the waters surrounding Wye Island as well as many other brackish water paddling environments in the Chesapeake Bay region. What you are witnessing is a cownose ray or group of cownose rays uncovering their favorite food, soft shell clams (they crush the shells with powerful dental plates), or possibly mating. Often they seem to just be playing. Possessing wings with a span up to three feet they can "fly" through the water at breakneck speeds. The sharklike fins you see zooming past are the tips of the wings breaking the surface.

The cownose ray is a nonbony fish, such as a shark, called cartilaginous fish. Double heads are another name for the cownose due to an indentation around the snout giving the appearance of having an upper and lower head region. They have skeletons made of cartilage and are quite primitive. Beware of their stinging spines located at the base of the tail.

Cownose rays are brownish on top and yellowish white on the bottom and their skin is smooth like a catfish. They range from New England to Brazil and reside in both the Caribbean and the Gulf of Mexico. Keep an eye out for them and be amazed. *—M.S.*

camping area and you have to walk through the group campsite to get to the pit toilet or to go for a hike. Please respect the campers and disturb them as little as possible.

Make sure to acquire a map from the Department of Natural Resources. It will have details about all the rest areas and the names of all the creeks.

A few words of caution: At times, boat traffic can be heavy. There are many bends in the waters surrounding Wye Island. Take care to paddle in the coves and be aware of the channels where most boats must navigate. It is easy to meander out into the path of an oncoming boat without realizing it. Try and pick a narrow area to make a crossing. Also, beware of poison ivy…it thrives on the banks of Wye Island.

The Department of Natural Resources is in the process of printing a map of land and water trails for Wye Island. As of this writing the final proof has been reviewed and the map is going to print. Go to www.dnr.state.md.us or call 410-260-8186 to request a map. For specific information call Wye Island directly: 410-827-7577.

22. *Tilghman Island*

Length: Circumnavigation is almost 10 miles. Add mileage if you paddle deep into Blackwalnut Cove.

Put-in site: Tilghman Harbor on Tilghman Island. No bathroom facilities. Please do not park in front of boat slips. These are for folks renting the slips. Keep off the grass and be conscious that folks choose to live on Tilghman for its serenity and appreciate paddlers who do not invade.

Driving Directions: From the Chesapeake Bay Bridge take 50E. Exit onto MD 322/Easton Parkway, and then exit onto MD 33. Follow past St. Michael's until it ends on Tilghman Island. After crossing the Knapp Narrows bridge onto Tilghman Island continue to Dogwood Harbor Road and turn left. Go to the left side of the harbor to small boat ramp and find parking. Do not park in any spaces in front of boat slips; these are for boat slip renters. Once you unload your gear, you may need to park on the other side of the harbor…to the right as you enter from the road.

TILGHMAN ISLAND is a sleepy small town that has maintained a relaxed atmosphere. In Tilghman Harbor sit the modern day workboats of the local waterman as well as a couple of skipjacks, testimony to the heyday of the oyster. The beauty of Tilghman is that it is away from the hustle and bustle of popular tourist destinations like St. Michael's. The paddling is much more serene with a great deal less boat traffic than other similar places. It is also a favorite paddling destination because its waters offer an expansive view of either the confluence of Harris Creek, Broad Creek, and the Choptank River on the east side or the open Chesapeake Bay on the west side.

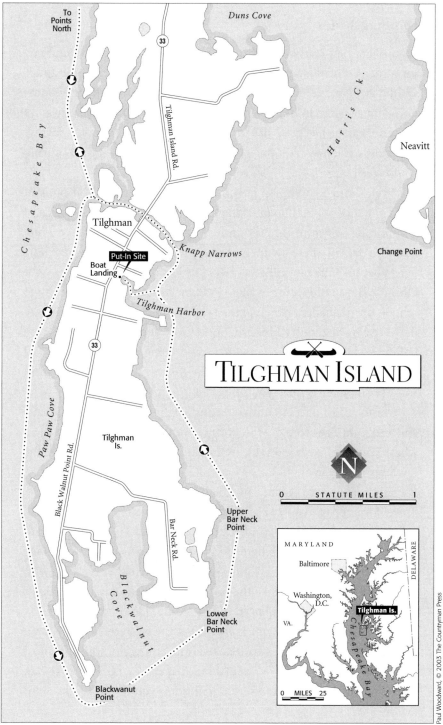

To Points North

Duns Cove

33

Tilghman Island Rd.

Chesapeake Bay

Harris Ck.

Neavitt

Tilghman

Knapp Narrows

Put-In Site

Boat Landing

Tilghman Harbor

Change Point

33

Paw Paw Cove

Black Walnut Point Rd.

Tilghman Is.

TILGHMAN ISLAND

N

0   STATUTE MILES   1

Upper Bar Neck Point

Bar Neck Rd.

Blackwalnut Cove

Lower Bar Neck Point

Blackwanut Point

MARYLAND

Baltimore

Washington, D.C.

VA.

DELAWARE

Tilghman Is.

Chesapeake Bay

0   MILES   25

Paul Woodward, © 2003 The Countryman Press

Paddling Notes

From Tilghman Harbor paddle north or south. Try and time your adventure to coincide with favorable tidal flow and wind. In the summer wind usually blows from the southwest. As mentioned above circumnavigating Tilghman Island is approximately a 10-mile trip. Some days the water can be like glass and so still you feel you are not even moving. Other days you may fight the wind and struggle at certain times during your voyage.

Even though Tilghman Island is somewhat developed it can still boast of a nice population of osprey, great blue herons, kingfishers, and a multitude of fish. You never know what you might see. Once while leading a day trip there I witnessed an osprey dive-bombing a great blue heron because the heron had gotten a little close to the osprey's nest. Observe the shallows for oysters and bait fish. Often there are huge schools of menhaden, which in the late summer and early autumn are devoured by aggressive bluefish. Sometimes the water appears to be boiling as the menhaden attempt to escape. Bring your fishing pole and cast a white or yellow buck tail into the frenzy and get ready to broil some fresh bluefish when you get home.

For the most part circumnavigating Tilghman is a relaxing paddle and a straightforward trip, with great views and beaches here and there where you can take breaks. Please be careful to not trespass as all the land is privately owned.

From Tilghman Harbor paddle left or north onto Harris Creek. Travel for approximately ½ mile and turn left (west) into Knapp Narrows. This is the small gap of water you crossed as you drove onto Tilghman Island. Be sharp here. Because this is such a narrow area for water to pass it gets squeezed and speeds up. It can either be going with or against you depending on the tide. Many powerboats and sailboats use the narrows so you will need to stay to one side.

To circumnavigate turn left (south) at the western side of Knapp Narrows. From this point to Blackwalnut Point, the southernmost point of Tilghman Island, is about 4 miles of exposed Chesapeake Bay. This is where the wind will affect you most. As you round Blackwalnut

Point you begin to enter the Choptank River. From here you can explore Blackwalnut Cove or head around to Lower Bar Neck Point and on up to return to Tilghman Harbor. From Blackwalnut Point to the harbor is close to 4 miles if you play it safe and stay near shore.

If you want to explore some beaches and not be committed to making it all the way around Tilghman, head right (north) at the western end of Knapp Narrows. Be wary of boat traffic as you cross the narrows. Once through Knapp Narrows you will be on the Chesapeake Bay. Keep to the shore. You are no longer paddling along Tilghman Island, but rather the mainland of the peninsula. There are some nice beaches along the way as you head north, and you can get the feel of paddling open water with the protection of the shore nearby. Two close creeks, Back and Front Creeks, can be explored along the way.

Paddling north you will see Coaches, Poplar, and Jefferson Islands 1 mile or so off shore to the west. It is a very tempting place to paddle to, and an easy float if weather conditions cooperate. However, the danger lies in the boat traffic passing between the island and the mainland. For a kayaker it is risky to go across. Powerboats come up much quicker than you realize. If you plan to cross, do it during the week. The channel to these islands sees a good deal of traffic on the weekends.

If you desire a short paddle just hang along the shore until you are ready to return and follow your tracks back.

You can also paddle up Harris Creek on the Choptank side if the wind is too strong on the bay. Just paddle past Knapp Narrows on your way out from Tilghman Harbor and explore Duns, Waterhole, and Briary Coves. There is a little more development on this side of the peninsula, but nice paddling all the same.

23. *Oxford/Tred Avon River*

Length: 6 to 12 miles

Put-in Site: Boat landing near Bellevue-Oxford Ferry

Driving Directions: *From Annapolis (the scenic route).* Follow US 50 east to MD 33 (to St. Michael's). Take MD 33 to MD 329.

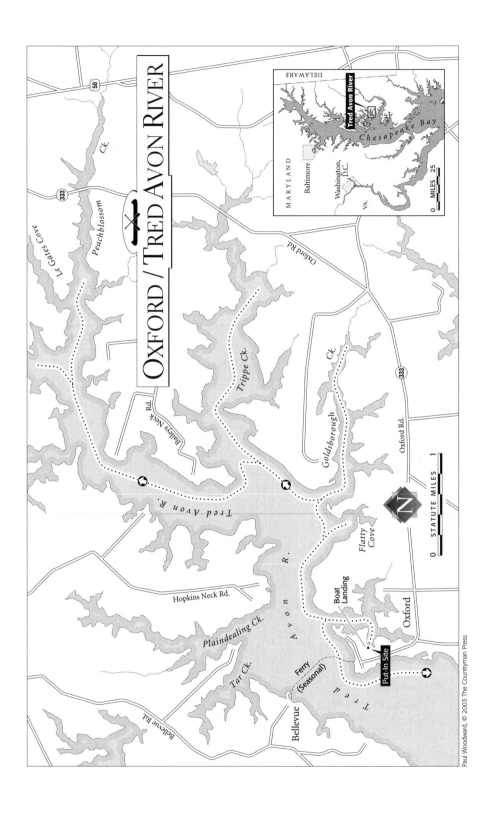

OXFORD / TRED AVON RIVER

MARYLAND

Baltimore

Washington, D.C.

VA.

DELAWARE

Tred Avon River

Chesapeake Bay

0 MILES 25

50

333

Le Gates Cove

Peachblossom Ck.

Oxford Rd.

Trippe Ck.

Baileys Neck Rd.

Goldsborough Ck.

333

Oxford Rd.

Tred Avon R.

Avon R.

Hopkins Neck Rd.

Plaindealing Ck.

Tar Ck.

Bellevue Rd.

Flatty Cove

Boat Landing

Put-In Site

Ferry (Seasonal)

Bellevue

Oxford

Tred Avon R.

N

0 STATUTE MILES 1

Paul Woodward, © 2003 The Countryman Press

Look for and follow signs to Bellevue-Oxford Ferry. Once on MD 329 it is less than 1 mile to Bellevue Road. Turn right onto Bellevue Road. Stay on Bellevue Road all the way to the Ferry landing (do not take Ferry Neck Road). Take the ferry across the Tred Avon River to Oxford. From the ferry landing in Oxford turn left onto East Strand. Stay on Strand till you just pass the Tred Avon Condos on the right. Turn into the gravel parking lot on the right just past the condos and park for the day. (The Bellvue-Oxford ferry, believed to be the oldest privately operated ferry in the United States, makes the trip across the Tred Avon River to Bellevue, every 25 minutes. The ferry runs from 7:00 AM to 9:00 PM Monday through Friday and 9:00 AM to 9:00 PM Saturday and Sunday during the summer months; 7:00 AM to sunset Monday through Friday and 9:00 AM to sunset Saturday and Sunday during spring and fall. The ferry does not operate in December, January, or February. Fares are $5.50 for car and passenger one way ($9.00 round trip), plus .50 for each extra passenger. Walk-ons can cross for $1.25, bicyclists pay $2.50, and motorcyclists pay $3.50.

From Annapolis: the quicker route. Cross Chesapeake Bay Bridge and stay on US 50E. Exit onto MD 322/Easton Parkway, and then exit onto MD 333 South. Drive for 11 miles to Oxford. Continue on this road as it bends to the right, becoming North Morris St. At the end of town, take a right on East Strand Rd. Stay on Strand until you pass the Tred Avon Condos on the right. Turn in the gravel parking lot on the right, just past the condos and park for the day.

OXFORD is situated at the confluence of the Choptank and Tred Avon Rivers in Talbot County. From this point, gazing southwest, you can view the wide-open space where the Choptank meets the Chesapeake. In the opposite direction lies the beautiful shoreline of the Tred Avon. Oxford was recognized by the Maryland Assembly in 1683 and is considered one of the oldest towns in the state. By 1694 Oxford and Annapolis were the only towns in Maryland approved by the Maryland Assembly as ports authorized for import and export. Since then Oxford has experienced a succession of economic growth and stagnant times.

Shipping, tobacco, oysters, shipbuilding, and now tourism have shaped Oxford's economy and population.

Oxford is still a quiet and beautiful small town and a great place to visit for a paddle on a lazy Sunday afternoon. It is also a favorite destination or stopping point for many cyclists. Just as often folks enjoy including Oxford on a driving tour of the eastern shore. On a weekend one can drive to St. Michael's and Tilghman Island and come back through St. Michael's and board the Bellvue/Oxford ferry across the Tred Avon River into Oxford.

Paddling Notes

Launch from the small beach just behind the parking lot into the harbor there. Paddle straight ahead into Town Creek. If you head to the right you can explore the back side of Oxford from the water. Head left and you will be on the Tred Avon shortly. Decide before you leave the harbor to either paddle south on the Tred Avon or north. Paddling south will bring you along the waterfront of Oxford and to the Choptank if you go that far. Traveling north will take you up the Tred Avon into more protected waters and, for the most part, less developed, non-bulkheaded shores.

If you decide to go north, go ahead and cross Town Creek as you leave the harbor area. Being on the north side of the creek as you approach the Tred Avon will help you avoid boat traffic coming in. At the Tred Avon, head right and keep near the shore on your right. You will pass by banks about 4 feet tall with some accessible beach depending on tide level. Keep an eye out for gray fox. Occasionally they can be spotted on the beach and in some of the holes in the bank. One day we saw four fox pups playing on the beach—they quickly scattered into one of their holes. Beautiful sight

Continue on along the shore and paddle in and out of the coves. The first you come to will be Flatty Cove. Along the way you will pass some easily sloping beaches and some sturdy salt marsh where you can rest or take lunch. If there is a nice breeze to keep the bugs away, get out on the marsh and explore. There are salt meadow hay, scat from herons and gulls, and signs of mammalian activity all through the area. Notice the transition from the saltwater marsh to the dryer forested land as you hike inward. (Be careful not to trespass.) Pine forests line the back of some of the marshlands. Find a quiet comfortable spot, lie down, and relax in the quiet.

Keep going. There are miles of shoreline and creeks and coves. After Flatty Cove you will come to Goldsborough Creek. At the point on the left as you enter is a gravel beach good for taking a break and a great place to swim. You will need to walk out a bit to get into water above your head. Nice beachcombing here as well. Further up the creek is beautiful, but you will see some development on both sides, but mostly on the right. Still, this is a nice paddle and worth the trip to the headwater. You have traveled about 4 miles when you reach the headwater of Goldsborough Creek. Past the point at the beginning of Goldsborough Creek few options exist to hop out of the kayak.

You can paddle up the Tred Avon as far as you like. I recommend staying on the east side due to a great deal of boat traffic up and down the main channel. The river is quite wide and the wind can be mighty strong due to the fetch (the amount of open area across which wind travels and picks up speed). Past Goldsborough Creek, staying to your right you will paddle into Trippe Creek. The Tred Avon is straight north from Goldsborough Creek. If you plan to paddle further up the Tred Avon make sure and do your crossing of Trippe Creek from a safe place. (Check out the *ADC Talbot County Street Map Book* for a better picture of the area.)

Upon your return, if you have the energy, you can paddle past Town Creek and head out to the mouth of the Tred Avon and even onto the Choptank. You will cross a channel at Town Creek where there can be a lot of boat traffic. Be careful. To your left will be the shoreline of Oxford and eventually the Bellevue/Tred Avon ferry landing. Just after the ferry landing you will round a point. Round the point, paddle a mile or so and you will come to a nice park. With some effort and not too high a tide you can leave your kayak among the rocks and take a break at the park. The park is on Morris Street (MD 333) where you can grab a sandwich and use the bathroom. The park itself is a great place to picnic and stare at the bigger boats out on the water.

This is the trip I typically take when leading a group. However we rarely make it to the park since groups typically travel slower than one or two people.

One could travel the Tred Avon all the way to Easton, MD. Hugging the shore and playing it safe, that trip is at least 8 miles one way. You could do a shuttle for such a trip. Or you could paddle into the Choptank. Keep in mind this is getting into open water paddling and wind can be a big factor. Again, keep close to shore.

For more information on the town of Oxford see these web sites: www.baydreaming.com/oxford.htm; and www.riverheritage.org/Riverguide/Trips/html/a_landing_at_oxford.html.

For information on other recreational activities call Talbot County Recreation and Parks: 410-822-2955.

24. *Taylor's Island Wildlife Management Area*

Length: Up to 8 to 10 miles for the described trip.

Put-in Site: Smithville Bridge (over Beaverdam Creek) off Smithville Road near Cambridge, Maryland.

Driving Directions: From Annapolis cross the Chesapeake Bay Bridge and head east on US 50. Follow US 50 over the Choptank River into Cambridge, MD. Go to MD 16/Gypsy Hill Road and turn right. MD 16 will take you all the way to Smithville Road. (You will pass through the small town of Church Creek. Slow down.) Just before the Taylors Island bridge, turn left on Smithville Road. (If you cross the bridge you have gone too far.) Follow Smithville Road until you come to a small blacktop parking lot on the right just before the bridge spanning Beaverdam Creek. Park here. This is the only boat landing on Smithville Road so it should be easy to find.

TAYLOR'S ISLAND WILDLIFE MANAGEMENT AREA (WMA), which encompasses 1,114 acres, is contiguous with the 27,000 acres that make up the Blackwater National Wildlife Refuge and the 21,000 acres of the Fishing Bay WMA. Together these protected lands make up a huge block of

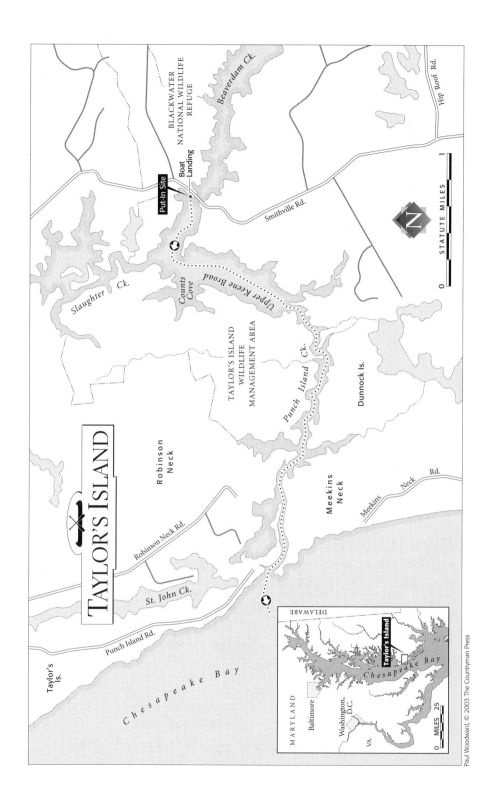

TAYLOR'S ISLAND

BLACKWATER NATIONAL WILDLIFE REFUGE

Beaverdam Ck.

Hip Roof Rd.

Boat Landing

Put-In Site

Smithville Rd.

Slaughter Ck.

Counts Cove

Upper Keene Broad

TAYLOR'S ISLAND WILDLIFE MANAGEMENT AREA

Punch Island Ck.

Dunnock Is.

Robinson Neck

Meekins Neck

Meekins Neck Rd.

Robinson Neck Rd.

St. John Ck.

Taylor's Is.

Punch Island Rd.

Chesapeake Bay

N

STATUTE MILES

0   1

MARYLAND

Baltimore

Washington, D.C.

VA.

DELAWARE

Taylor's Island

Chesapeake Bay

0   MILES   25

Paul Woodward, © 2003 The Countryman Press

brackish water tidal marshland, rivers and creeks, forests, and fresh-water ponds. In addition private lands that are mostly undeveloped with very small populations surround these national and state treasures. This area is perfect for the thousands of different critters that inhabit the area and are dependent on it for survival. Bald eagles and osprey, once on the brink of extinction, have made a serious comeback thanks in part to this acreage. The Delmarva fox squirrel has a fighting chance here and thousands of birds, mammals, reptiles, and fish depend on the pristine environment for survival. You may not see another person all day while paddling here, especially during the week.

Ironically, you do not even need to touch Taylor's Island during this paddle, but you could if you wanted to depending on where you take breaks and your direction of travel. What I like most about this trail is that you can be on the open waters of the Chesapeake Bay in only 4 miles if you paddle the most direct route.

Paddling Notes

Be sure to bring a compass just in case. Bring a map too. Purchase some topographic maps or use the *Dorchester County Street Map Book* from ADC ("The Map People"). Here, the salt marsh often looks the same coming or going. From the put-in spot paddle west (northwest) on Beaverdam Creek for about ¾ mile away from the bridge. (Please avoid paddling the opposite direction under the bridge due to nesting bald eagles.) You will intersect with Upper Keen Broad Creek to the south and Slaughter Creek to the north. Head south. Upper Keen Broad Creek opens up pretty wide. On the right you will pass Counts Cove. Keep to the most obvious direction of travel. The creek begins to narrow a little more than a mile from its union with Beaverdam Creek. Paddle another almost ½ mile and this waterway changes names again to Punch Island Creek. Punch Island Creek will dump you onto the Chesapeake Bay after another 2 miles.

As you are paddling from the put-in toward the Chesapeake, the land to the right, from the put-in to Robinson Cove, is Fishing Bay WMA property and is therefore public property. This is about halfway down Punch Island Creek. Past Robinson Cove the land is private property as is the entire left shore as you paddle to the bay. Once you hit the Chesapeake Bay the shore north and south is private as well. So, please stay below the high-tide line when taking breaks on the Chesapeake shore.

Remember, the description above is the most direct route to the Chesapeake Bay. Any exploring of coves and guts will add more mileage. Just where Upper Keene Broad and Punch Island Creeks join there lays the confluence of Dunnock Island Creek. You can take a left into Dunnock Island Creek and in a ½ mile go right into Dunnock Slough. Paddle Dunnock Slough for almost 2 miles to return to Punch Island Creek. This route is basically a loop that will put you back into Punch Island Creek across from Robinson Cove. If the day is really windy consider this route. Because of the narrowness of these guts you may receive some protection. It will add about 1¾ mile to your trip one way. Double that if you take this route out and back, assuming, of course, that you stay on track. It can be somewhat of a maze. There are acres of guts and streams to explore on the way to the bay. You can paddle around islands up guts that end as ponds, and past well-established forests. The side trips are certainly worth the effort. Just know your ability, be aware of wind, weather, and tidal flow and make a solid plan. Wind and tide can really move the water in this area.

Once on the Chesapeake it is time to take a break and wonder at her beauty. On a warm day with a nice breeze you could take a nap. Stroll along the shoreline in search of some beached treasure (feel free to take some trash back with you and dispose of it properly). Beautiful oyster shells and twisted driftwood and entire trees (which are great benches for lunch) line the coast. Stare out into the bay and you may see the other side on a clear day. Punch Island Creek enters the Chesapeake Bay almost directly across from the famous Calvert Cliffs State Park. It is about 6 miles across the bay to Calvert Cliffs. If you are lucky you will witness one of the huge ships leaving or heading to Baltimore. Try and see what country it is from.

You can paddle north or south on the bay. Keep near the shore for safety and to avoid powerboats (although the chances are you will not see a soul). Heading north you paddle along the shore of Taylor's Island. At the northern point of Taylor's are James Island (not Jane's Island which is described in this guide), and the mouth of the little Choptank River. Head south from Punch Island Creek and you'll find Cattail Island, Boggs Gut, Big Tar Bay, and other interesting places.

One could paddle this area and the connecting protected lands for years. There are guts and creeks meandering through the land that can take you from Taylors Island WMA, through Blackwater NWR and into Fishing Bay WMA. That trip would need to be well planned, perhaps spending a night or two in the wilderness, and is beyond the scope of this book. But I want to give you an idea of how much beauty there is here.

This paddle offers solitude and serenity: Let's hope it stays that way.

For more information on the Taylor Island Wildlife Management Area call the Lecompe Wildlife Office: 410-376-3236.

25. *Blackwater National Wildlife Refuge*

Length: In and out of Coles Creek is about 5 miles. However there are numerous guts and ponds to explore and one can paddle all day. Another option is a 6-mile paddle one-way or 12 mile round trip. This is the Blackwater River Trail.

Put-in Site: Shorter's Wharf Landing on the Blackwater River.

Driving Directions: Shorter's Wharf landing: Expect a two-hour drive from Annapolis. From the Chesapeake Bay Bridge tollbooth at US 50 east it is approximately 50 miles to the first brown sign for the Blackwater National Wildlife Refuge. Take US 50 east until you cross the Choptank River and start looking for the brown sign. Follow the sign and turn right on MD 16 West (Wal-Mart on your right). After 2 miles on MD 16 you will take a left on Maple Dam Road (drive slow or you will miss it, the turn comes in less than 5 miles on MD 16), a Shell station is on the right. Follow Maple Dam Road through Blackwater Wildlife Refuge (you will pass signs to the visitor's center—consider stopping there for a trail map or other information). Stay on Maple Dam Road for approximately 13 miles. You will cross

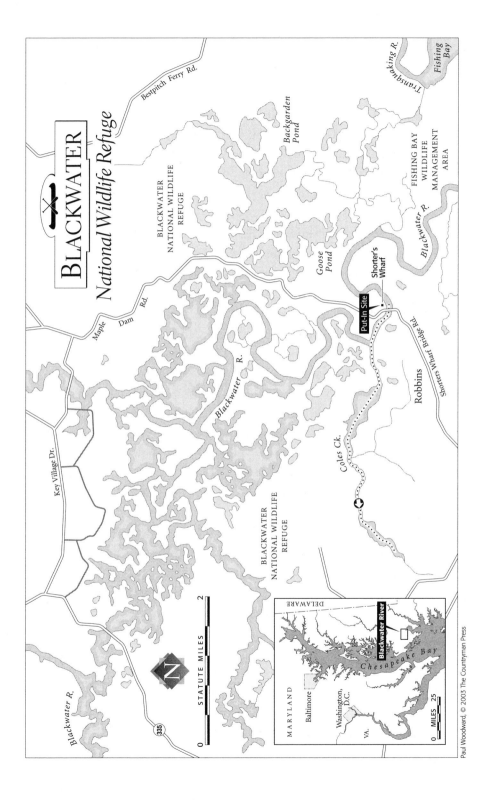

BLACKWATER
National Wildlife Refuge

Bestpitch Ferry Rd.

Backgarden Pond

BLACKWATER
NATIONAL WILDLIFE
REFUGE

Transquaking R.

Fishing Bay

FISHING BAY
WILDLIFE
MANAGEMENT
AREA

Goose Pond

Blackwater R.

Shorter's Wharf

Put-In Site

Maple Dam Rd.

Blackwater R.

Robbins

Shorters Wharf Bridge Rd.

Key Village Dr.

Coles Ck.

BLACKWATER
NATIONAL WILDLIFE
REFUGE

Blackwater R.

335

N

STATUTE MILES

0   2

DELAWARE

MARYLAND

Baltimore

Washington, D.C.

VA.

Blackwater River

Chesapeake Bay

0   MILES   25

Paul Woodward, © 2003 The Countryman Press

over the Blackwater River and the landing is on the right just
past the bridge.

BLACKWATER NATIONAL WILDLIFE REFUGE encompasses more than 27,000
acres of brackish tidal water and wetlands, evergreen and deciduous
forest, open fields, and impoundments of fresh water. It was established
in 1933 as a waterfowl sanctuary for birds migrating along the critical
Atlantic Flyway (a migratory bird route that stretches from Canada to
Florida).

The Blackwater National Wildlife Refuge is fed by the Blackwater
River and the Little Blackwater River. Both derive their names from the
acid-darkened water that flows in and around the refuge. In addition
to a wealth of wetlands, Blackwater is also home to more than 250 bird
species and three recovering species: the endangered Delmarva fox
squirrel, the recently de-listed migrant peregrine falcon, and the American bald eagle, which has been upgraded from endangered to threatened thanks to laws such as the Endangered Species Act.

Blackwater also boasts 35 species of reptiles and amphibians, tens
of thousands of geese and ducks during the peak migration periods,
and many resident mammals including white-tailed deer, sika deer (an
Asian elk), foxes, otters, and raccoons. The bald eagle population is a
source of great pride at Blackwater Refuge and has grown into the
largest concentration of bald eagles in the eastern United States, north
of Florida.

Paddling Blackwater can be like finding your way through a maze.
The guts and bays twist and turn and everything can look the same
coming or going, so be sure to bring a map and compass. However, if
you want to paddle an area where you can feel you are the only person
on earth, Blackwater is the place to be.

Paddling Notes

From Shorter's Wharf up Coles Creek and back: A new boat landing has
recently been completed on the Blackwater River at Shorter's Wharf. It
is on the southwest side of the Blackwater River. The old ramp, on the

Enjoying the open feel of the Blackwater River

other side, is constantly under water at high tide and because of its location much silt is continuously dropped there. Often paddlers would be in mud up to the calves while launching.

This area is tidal, as is most of the Blackwater Wildlife Refuge. From my experience the tide changes are hard to predict. So, be prepared to paddle against the tide and wind sometime during your trip and possibly the entire trip. Along your paddle there are numerous guts to explore up into the salt marsh. Places to get out and stretch or enjoy lunch are few. But, with a keen eye and the willingness to get your feet wet and possibly muddy, one can take a break in the marsh. Also, try and find already used take-outs to lessen environmental impact.

From Shorter's Wharf go left or upstream on the Blackwater River for ½ mile and take another left at the first big gut. This is Coles Creek. For the first ½ mile or so you are paddling through an obvious tidal creek environment. Coles Creek eventually opens up and you can experience paddling in a pond or lakelike environment. Be ready to deal with some wind. Keep paddling and as the creek narrows again there is a good place to take a break on the right. Keep an eye out for some old pilings in your path, this is your landmark. There is solid ground here and a good place to take lunch. Often there is an upturned boat where you can put out your spread.

Continue up Coles Creek another mile or so and it will eventually peter out. It is quite beautiful the entire way with no obvious signs of development. Eagles are often spotted during this paddle. Along the way there is a man-made gut you can explore. It is an interesting paddle because one can get the feeling of moving through a jungle since the vegetation towers over you.

At low tide your paddle and kayak will scrape bottom in the upper reaches of the creek. Be sure to escape before you run out of water due to tidal changes.

There are a couple of options as you head back that can add up to another 2½ miles to your trip. Take a good look at your map/chart. When you are in the pond area of Coles Creek, as you return, on the northern or left side, you will notice a gut. From the kayak it is difficult to see. It is just before the creek narrows again. This waterway can lead you back to the Blackwater River, but there are three paths you can take. All will put you on the Blackwater further north than where you entered Coles Creek. Paddling here is magical. The guts get very narrow, the wind stops, it gets quiet (even more quiet). The temperature changes and one begins to notice the little things. It is easy to lose yourself in the sway of the tall cordgrass and wild rice. Small fish scurry to escape you, the predator. From the corner of your eye you'll see the petite nests of marsh wrens. Up ahead you notice a muskrat disappearing into the marsh.

Be sure and take a topographic map and compass with you. It is easy to get turned around. One of our guides ended up paddling a little longer than planned one day. The wind was strong and the threat of rain and lightning loomed above. He returned with his group just as the sky opened up and lightning started to crack. Everyone was beat. Be on the lookout for bald eagles, herons, egrets, kingfishers, and other birds. Otter and muskrat are sometimes spotted, and nutria are often spotted (see page 60).

Stop at the visitor's center and pick up the new Blackwater Trail maps just completed by the Friends of Blackwater. This path is described as well as two others. The map is an excellent guide. There are

Great Blue Herons (*Ardea herodias*)

You may see several different types of herons in the Chesapeake region. We have seen the green heron, great egret, snowy egret, and black-crowned and yellow-crowned night herons. But, the heron most folks spot during the day is the great blue heron. They are huge wading birds 39 to 52 inches tall with a wingspan of up to 70 inches. The blue heron quietly and slowly wades in the shallows ever ready to spear an unsuspecting fish or crab. Since they're pretty shy it is a treat to get fairly close to one. From a distance you can enjoy great detail by using binoculars and kayaks can be paddled in a very stealthy manner. It is beautiful to watch them walk through the water. Their feet are not webbed, but are three long toes with claws and they spread out to disperse their weight allowing them to wade in areas with fairly soft mud. When great blue herons are concentrating on their prey they will often turn their heads to the side and then strike like lightning to snag the next piece of dinner.

Great blues are also spotted up high on tree branches and flying overhead. They nest up high in trees and if you can spot a rookery in the early spring before the leaves have returned it is easy to see where Dr. Seuss got his inspiration. After the hatchlings have flown the coop and there is no chance of disturbing the herons in the rookery, take a walk under one and comb through the remains of their dinners. You usually need to wait until the fall to do this. Absolutely amazing. Besides ground crab shells, whole claws and other boluses from the sea, I have found the rib cage of a baby muskrat. Take a look up at the nest and marvel at their size and ingenuity.

Occasionally you will turn a corner in your kayak and spook a heron into flight. At times they will let out this indescribable croak—my bird guidebook describes it as "a harsh guttural squawk." If you are paddling at night and suddenly hear this exclamation without seeing the heron, be ready to catch your breath. After take-off great blues fly with their necks folded.

The typical great blue heron is grayish with a yellow bill. When mature they often have a blackish tuft of feathers extending off the back of the skull which is an extension of a black stripe that starts at the beak, passes through the eye and connects with the tuft. The upper and middle part of the neck can be a rust color with grayish feathers hanging where the neck connects to the body. There is often a black splotch on the body just before the wings. The legs are greenish-yellow. They inhabit lakes, ponds, rivers, marshes, and bays and their primary food are fish and frogs. They also feed on small mammals, reptiles and occasionally birds. They are colonial nesters and lay 3–5 pale greenish-blue eggs. Most migrate south in the fall. —*M.S.*

many more miles of paddling to be had in the Blackwater Refuge.

For more information please see www.blackwater.fws.gov, U.S. Fish and Wildlife Service; or www.friendsofblackwater.org, Friends of Blackwater (there is even an Osprey Camera). Or call the Blackwater National Wildlife Refuge Visitor's Center: 410-228-2677.

26. *Transquaking River Loop Trail* (Part of the Fishing Bay *Wildlife Management Area Water Trail System*)

Length: 5 to 6 mile round trip on the Loop Trail.

Put-in Site: Bestpitch Road launch site on the Transquaking River. To obtain the Fishing Bay Water Trails map and other water trail maps go to: Maryland Department of Natural Resources: www.dnr.state.md.us or 410-543-6595.

Driving Directions: From Annapolis take US 50 east across the Chesapeake Bay Bridge. Follow US 50 east to Cambridge and continue through Cambridge to the Bucktown Road exit (also airport exit), on the right. Follow Bucktown Road south, approximately 6 miles to Bestpitch Ferry Road. Turn left onto Bestpitch Ferry Road and continue for approximately 4 miles to Bestpitch. Just before crossing the bridge at the Transquaking River turn right onto the Fishing Bay WMA boat launch entrance road and follow it to the launch area.

THE FISHING BAY WILDLIFE MANAGEMENT AREA (WMA) encompasses 21,000 acres of tidal marshlands with a few dispersed islands of loblolly pine. The area is managed by Maryland's Department of Natural Resources. Also involved in creating water trails in the area are the Dorchester County Department of Tourism and The Maryland Greenways Commission. Fishing Bay WMA is Maryland's largest publicly owned parcel of tidal wetlands and the state's largest wildlife management area.

The Fishing Bay WMA is connected with the 25,000 acres of preserved land that makes up the Blackwater National Wildlife Refuge which lies to the west. Further west is the Taylor Island WMA. Together this is the largest tract of land set aside in Maryland for wildlife. Also contiguous are many acres of private land that is mostly undeveloped.

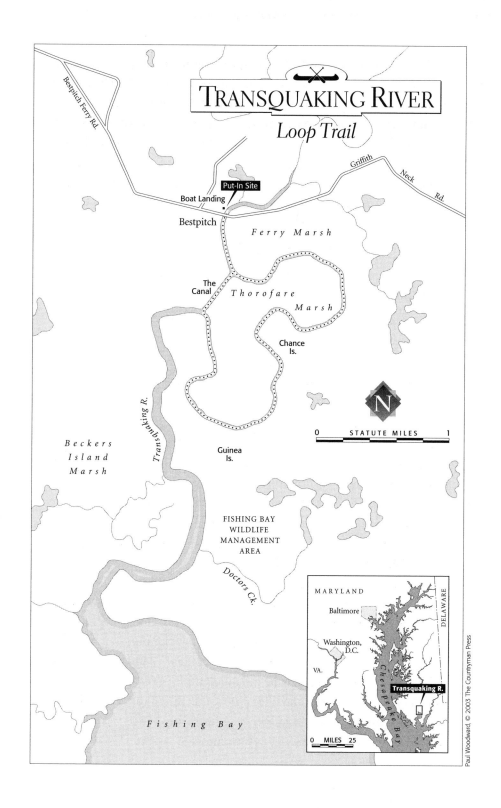

TRANSQUAKING RIVER
Loop Trail

Bestpitch Ferry Rd.

Griffith

Neck

Rd.

Put-In Site

Boat Landing

Bestpitch

Ferry Marsh

The Canal

Thorofare

Marsh

Chance Is.

Transquaking R.

N

0 STATUTE MILES 1

Beckers Island Marsh

Guinea Is.

FISHING BAY WILDLIFE MANAGEMENT AREA

Doctors Ck.

Fishing Bay

MARYLAND

Baltimore

Washington, D.C.

VA.

DELAWARE

Transquaking R.

Chesapeake Bay

0 MILES 25

Paul Woodward, © 2003 The Countryman Press

This part of the eastern shore hosts a great deal of wildlife. Eagles, osprey, rails, herons, egrets, hawks, migratory shore birds, ducks, geese, and overwintering waterfowl depend on this oasis of natural habitat. Mammals such as the white-tailed deer, sika deer, muskrat, nutria (see page 60), river otter, raccoons and squirrels make this area home.

Fishing Bay is the headwater of Tangier Sound which surrounds a chain of islands that stretch from just south of Fishing Bay down into northern Virginia. Fishing Bay is fed by many small creeks and guts as well as the Blackwater and Transquaking River. Both of these rivers flow from protected and mostly pristine environments.

Paddling Notes

From the launch area paddle south or away from the bridge on the Transquaking River. In just under ⅓ mile you will be at "The Canal." Either turn right into "The Canal," or continue on the Transquaking. If you turn into "The Canal" it is another almost ⅓ mile straight shot back to the Transquaking a little further downstream. At this intersection turn left and you will be paddling upstream. (Downstream and upstream refer to the net water flow of the river. If the tide is coming up the river may seem to be flowing upstream. You may be paddling with the flow of the water and going upstream or you may be paddling against the current when you are paddling downstream. Be aware of the tidal changes in regard to how a river flows so you always know your direction of travel.) This section of the Transquaking is "The Loop" and the paddle is just over 4 miles back to the entrance of "The Canal." Keep on the Transquaking to return to the launch site, another ⅓ mile.

Along the way you will pass Chance Island and Guinea Island rising out of the marsh, two of the largest wooded islands in Fishing Bay WMA. These are good places to stretch your legs. You can get a good view of your surroundings from on top of these islands. The Nause-Waiwash Native American tribe inhabited these islands. Some of their members visit the area today. Please be respectful of the area. You may run across some oyster *middens* or piles of discarded oyster shells placed there by Native Americans for centuries.

There are a few guts or creeks off the Transquaking on the Loop path that you can explore. These are fun and easy to navigate during high tide, often narrow and switching back and forth. Paddling up these guts is magical because the wind gets blocked, the environment grows quiet, and you get the feeling you are the only person in the world. Be still for some time. Eventually all the sounds of the marsh that are there when humans are not begin to return. This can give the paddler an idea of what the marsh is like all the time, everyday.

For a longer paddle continue downstream past "The Canal," and make your way to the top of Fishing Bay. From the southern end of "The Canal" to Alabaster Point at the mouth of the Transquaking River is right at 4 miles. From here you can return or paddle around Fishing Bay. Fishing Bay is an open water environment and therefore you may be dealing with much stronger winds than in the more protected area from which you just ventured.

There are many, many miles of paddling in this area. So far the Department of Natural Resources has two official water trails for the Fishing Bay WMA. One is the Transquaking River Loop and the other is the Island Creek Trail. A waterproof, multicolored map of the Fishing Bay Water Trails is available through the DNR. If you want to do a pretty long shuttle with a friend, you could paddle from Bestpitch Road to the Island Creek Trail up to Elliot Island Road and take out. Keep in mind that these paddles can be quite strenuous due to the wind and current, and the marsh is basically a maze in which one can get lost very quickly. Bring a compass, a map, and leave a float plan with someone back home in case you are late in returning.

27. *The Pocomoke River and Nassawango Creek*

> **Length:** From the put-in up Nassawango Creek and return: 10 miles round-trip. From the put-in and north on the Pocomoke: 8 miles plus round-trip.
>
> **Put-in Site:** Byrd Park on the Pocomoke River in Snow Hill, Maryland. From here you can paddle up or down the

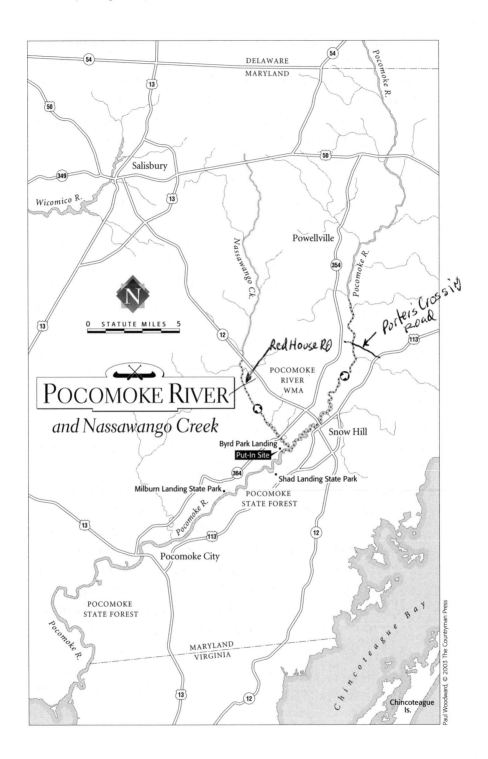

Pocomoke River and Nassawango Creek.

Driving Directions: *Byrd Park:* From the Chesapeake Bay Bridge follow US 50 East. East of Salisbury take US 13 South to MD 12 to Snow Hill. Follow MD 12 South for about 15 miles to Snow Hill. Immediately after crossing the bridge into Snow Hill turn right onto Market Street/US 113 & MD 12. Follow for a short time and turn right into Byrd Park. There is only a small street sign that marks Byrd Park. Follow park road around to the right to the boat landing. Expect a 2-hour drive from Annapolis.

Directions to the Pocomoke River Canoe Company in Snow Hill: Follow US 50 East. Just east of Salisbury take US 13 south to route MD 12 to Snow Hill. Once in Snow Hill look for a red, wooden building adjacent to the drawbridge over the Pocomoke River.

Directions to Red House Road: Follow directions above to Snow Hill, but turn right onto Red House Road before crossing the bridge over the Pocomoke. Go to the bridge over the Nassawango Creek.

Contact info and more: 410-632-3971 or 800-258-0905 and www.atbeach.com/amuse/md/canoe

---

IN 1971 the Pocomoke River was designated as Maryland's first Scenic and Wild River because it possesses "unique natural and scenic resources." Although the upper Pocomoke has had channels added to drain land for agricultural use and navigation, and the bottomland forests were harvested (mostly cypress and cedar for roof shingles), its wilderness is mostly intact due to the end of these practices and the miracle of regeneration.

What makes the Pocomoke River and Nassawango Creek so unique is how different it is from almost every other waterway in Maryland. It is often compared more to the Dismal Swamp in southern Virginia and North Carolina. A number of critters found here are not found elsewhere in Maryland, especially north of the Pocomoke. This environment is just what southern reptiles, amphibians and other residents of the wild need. More than 130 rare, threatened or endangered inhabitants have been identified here by the Maryland Department of Natural Resources.

Being a Louisiana native, I feel right at home on the Pocomoke

River. The water is deep black but quite clear...a contradictory statement, but dip your paddle and notice how easy it is to see. There is very little turbidity. Tannic acid leached from the cypress trees creates the black color but there seems to be little floating sediment. Of course, seasonal rains, farming, and development will affect visibility. On my last visit, however, the water was beautiful and crystal clear.

With huge cypress trees, the smell of fresh water, and hundreds of painted turtles, it feels like paddling deep in the swamps of southern Louisiana. On my last trip I saw eagles, herons, kingfishers...the only thing missing was the occasional gator. This place is just absolutely gorgeous, quiet and serene.

Paddling Notes

From Byrd Park on the Pocomoke, up Nassawango Creek and back
From Byrd Park landing head left (south) and paddle downstream on the Pocomoke River for 2 miles. Along the way you will pass Goat Island before you come to the mouth of Nassawango Creek (the first tributary you come to on the right or west side of the Pocomoke). Take your time paddling up the Nassawango. Savor every stroke as you gaze at the beauty surrounding you. After you pass under the first bridge (Nassawango Road) there are few signs of modern civilization. The creek begins to narrow. and the swamp and forest create a tunnel through which you must pass.

On warm days you will probably spot numerous turtles and a few snakes, mostly northern brown water snakes. They are not poisonous (no water moccasins in Maryland) and are harmless unless cornered. The next bridge you encounter is Red House Road. This is about as far as you can paddle and a great place to take a break. Red House Road is approximately 3 miles from the mouth of Nassawango Creek (depends on which map one uses). There is much meandering and you may feel that you will get lost. Just keep to the most obvious areas. There is only one way in and one way out. There are a couple of small feeder creeks that enter Nassawango, but do not seem to be navigable.

On the way upstream, after passing Nassawango Road, study the southern side of the creek. There is a small, almost hidden cove that curves into the bank. You can take a break here. The Nature Conservancy owns this area. In the 1970s the Nature Conservancy began acquiring land to create a regional preserve. At present almost 3,000 acres are part of the preservation program. Thanks to relatively little development on Nassawango as well as continued conservation efforts the creek is still considered wild and possesses the habitat that makes it so unique.

From Byrd Park, up Nassawango Creek to Red House Road and back is close to 12 miles. This can be a long trip if there is a good deal of wind. There is the option of doing a one-way trip. You could leave a vehicle at Red House Road and one at Byrd Park and paddle one way or the other. Or you could put in at Red House Road and paddle down and up Nassawango Creek. Another option is to have the folks at Pocomoke River Canoe Company shuttle you (see above for directions to Red House Road and info on Pocomoke River Canoe Company).

Byrd Park up the Pocomoke (or north and return)

From Byrd Park paddle right (north) up the Pocomoke. There is much paddling to be done going this way, however, water level will determine just how far you can make it. In less than a mile you will paddle under MD 365 or Snow Hill Road. Just past the bridge sits the Pocomoke River Canoe Company on the right. Paddling further, the Pocomoke continues to wind back and forth and there are small islands to pass around and perhaps some flooded wetlands to float over. You will eventually float below a power line and the Pocomoke begins to really narrow. The next bridge you come to is Porters Crossing Road, around 4 miles or so from Byrd Park. If water level permits paddle another 4 plus miles to Whiton Crossing Road. The Pocomoke begins to really narrow from this point on.

Again, this could be a long trip going out and back. At some point you will paddle against the current and probably some wind. If you would rather do a one-way trip you can do a shuttle yourself or hire the folks at Pocomoke River Canoe to do the shuttle for you and take the hassle out of the day.

As with the Nassawango Creek route, this is a beautiful paddle filled with cypress, turtles, kingfishers, osprey, eagles, and all kinds of small birds. Lush forests and wetlands filled with yellow pond lily or spatterdock abound.

Keep in mind that the folks at Potomac River Canoe allow paddlers to put in from their store, which is about ½ of a mile north of Byrd Park.

For a decent map acquire The Pocomoke River Greenway, prepared for The Maryland Greenways Commission by Greenways and Resource Planning, Maryland Department of Natural Resources (410-974-3589).

28. *Janes Island Water Trail*

Length: Several trail options ranging from 2 miles to 12 miles. (Overnight kayak camping trails available as well, contact park or acquire information at the DNR web site—see page 162.)

Put-in Site: Janes Island State Park marina and boat launch.

Driving Directions: From the Baltimore or Washington area take US 50 east over the Chesapeake Bay Bridge to Salisbury. After passing through Salisbury take Rt. 13 south. Exit from Rt.13 onto Rt. 413 (right turn) and follow signs to Crisfield. Turn right onto Plantation Road and follow for about 1 mile to the park entrance. From Norfolk, take US 13 across the Chesapeake Bay Bridge tunnel to Pocomoke City. Follow MD 557 to MD 413 south and proceed for about 5 miles. Turn right onto Plantation Road and follow for about 1 mile to the park entrance.

WITHIN JANES ISLAND STATE PARK is an established water trail system called, you guessed it, Janes Island Water Trail. The Maryland Greenways Commission coordinates the creation of a statewide system of greenways and water trails and has created this trail along with others. Jane's Island is truly a playground for kayakers. If you are into wildlife, tidal water, the smell of the salt marsh, meandering creeks, beautiful sandy beaches, and expansive views of the Chesapeake's Tangier Sound, Janes Island is the place to spend some time.

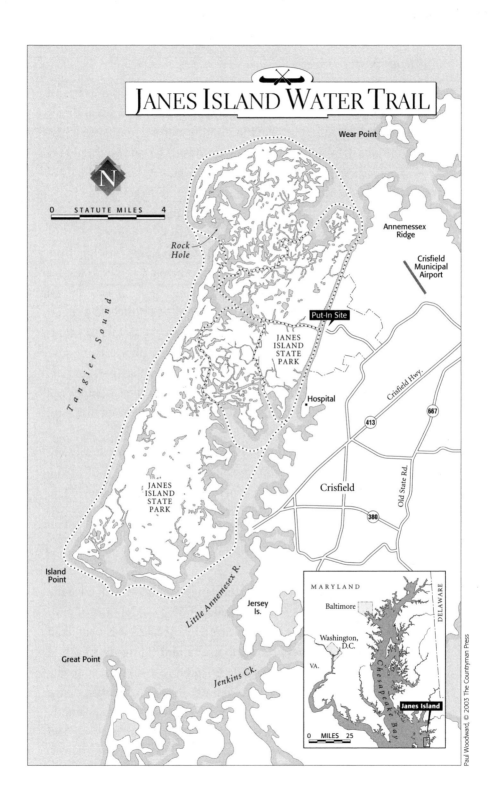

JANES ISLAND WATER TRAIL

Wear Point

N

0 STATUTE MILES 4

Rock Hole

Annemessex Ridge

Crisfield Municipal Airport

Put-In Site

Tangier Sound

JANES ISLAND STATE PARK

Hospital

Crisfield Hwy.

413

667

Old State Rd.

JANES ISLAND STATE PARK

Crisfield

380

Island Point

Little Annemesex R.

Jersey Is.

Great Point

Jenkins Ck.

MARYLAND

Baltimore

DELAWARE

Washington, D.C.

VA.

Chesapeake Bay

Janes Island

0 MILES 25

Paddling Notes

When you arrive at the park ask them for a copy of the Janes Island Water Trail map. Not only does it display all the marked trails and meandering guts, it is full of information on the cultural and natural history of the area. (If you are into fishing from your kayak you should try here.) There are six established water trails in this system and loads of creek and coves to meander through if you choose to get off the trails. All six begin from the marina and boat launch and are distinguished by color: Yellow (2½ miles), Blue (2½ miles), Black (3½ miles), Red (4 miles), Green (6¼ miles), and Brown (12½ miles) trails. Paddling time predictions printed on the maps are based on a pace of 2½ miles per hour.

Almost 2,900 acres of marsh and shore land are protected at Janes Island. A great variety of paddling conditions are possible. The island possesses tight meandering guts, open ponds, larger tidal streams, and open water shore paddling. For the most part the water trails and inland paddling can be protected from wind. Out on the Chesapeake's Tangier Sound you can experience tranquil paddling or challenging small surf conditions.

The Brown trail takes you all the way around the island. You will have the feeling of paddling open water for more than half of the journey. On the way you will pass pristine, secluded beaches, "The Stack" or Old Island Chimney, the last remains of a once thriving fish processing plant, and small community. You will take in the view of Crisfield and the dock area used to ferry folks back and forth to Smith and Tangier Islands.

During your paddle in and around Janes Island you will have the opportunity to see a variety of wildlife depending on the time of year, your luck, and your ability to paddle quietly. Because it is protected and the marsh and beaches are able to evolve and change in a natural unimpeded way, Janes Island is quite hospitable to a variety of critters. Do not be surprised if you see diamondback terrapin (see page 138), osprey, bald eagles, northern harrier, brown pelicans, Canada geese, mallards, great blue herons (see page 161), cattle egret, and snowy egret year-round. In October expect to observe in addition to the above, whistling swan, oldsquaw, common goldeneye, and bufflehead.

Fishing is usually fruitful in the waters surrounding Janes Island. Flounder, striped bass (rockfish), croaker, Norfolk spot, and speckled and gray trout are abundant. Also keep an eye out for the ever-stalking blue crab (see page 185).

As you paddle through the interior of Janes Island, you may notice a smell similar to rotten eggs or sulfur. That smell is the result of anaerobic (without oxygen) decomposition. What is decomposing is dead plant and animal matter. As it breaks down it turns into soil that in turn accepts the seeds of other marsh plants and continues the cycle of marsh building. Plants 2 to 6 feet tall named saltmarsh cordgrass that grow near the waters edge will often shroud you. In from the edge you will find salt meadow hay. This plant is a beautiful green and invites one to take a break and relax in the sun.

If possible, take some time and explore the salt marsh by foot. Be careful to avoid causing erosion. Step on the more firm areas and avoid concentrating foot traffic in one spot. You may notice the earth moving below you. The salt marsh is merely a giant sponge held together by the roots of the plants whose growth the marsh supports. Bend down and spread some of the marsh grass apart. You may find some tiny snails called "coffee bean" snails that thrive in this environment. You may also notice fiddler crabs scurrying for cover as you come across a mud flat.

All in all Janes Island is an excellent paddle. With its variety of trails, the state park to camp in, local hotels and bed & breakfasts, and excellent seafood restaurants in Crisfield, a kayaker's every wish could come true.

Alert: during the summer months be ready to deal with mosquitoes and biting green head flies. Head nets and repellent are a must.

29. *Assateague Island National Seashore: Chincoteague and Sinepuxent Bay*

Length: Many options exist so you can paddle as much or as little as you choose.

Put-in Site: Old Ferry Landing in Assateague Island National Seashore (check-in at the Ranger Station for a park map and leave a trip plan with them).

Driving Directions: *From Annapolis:* Take US 50 East, through Salisbury to MD 611 South (Just before Ocean City). Follow MD 611 south to Assateague Island, cross the bridge over Chincoteague and Sinepuxent Bays to Assateague Island. Once on the Island take a right into Assateague Island's National Seashore, the first right turn once you get on the island. There is a $4 "day use" entrance fee at the gatehouse for parking. Turn right at the sign for Old Ferry Landing and follow to the end.

ALTHOUGH ASSATEAGUE ISLAND and the bays trapped by it are not in the Chesapeake Bay Watershed, one cannot write about sea kayaking in Maryland without mentioning this area. Assateague Island is a barrier island between the Atlantic Ocean and the mainland. This geology allows for a unique and important ecosystem. From the northern tip of Assateague Island to the Maryland/Virginia line and on down to the southernmost tip in Virginia lies a beautiful expanse of salt marsh and pine forests on the inland or western side of the island. On the eastern side lie the pristine beaches of the Atlantic that make up the Assateague National Seashore. The Maryland side of Assateague Island is called the Assateague Island National Seashore and is maintained for recreational use as well as wildlife habitat. The Virginia side is called the Chincoteague National Wildlife Refuge and is mostly maintained as wildlife habitat. Fortunately this barrier island was saved from development and the parks established in 1943.

Thanks to establishment of these areas migratory and nesting birds have a better chance at surviving our continuously developing world. A quick trip to Ocean City will fill any nature-lover with gratitude toward the National Park Service and their forward thinking.

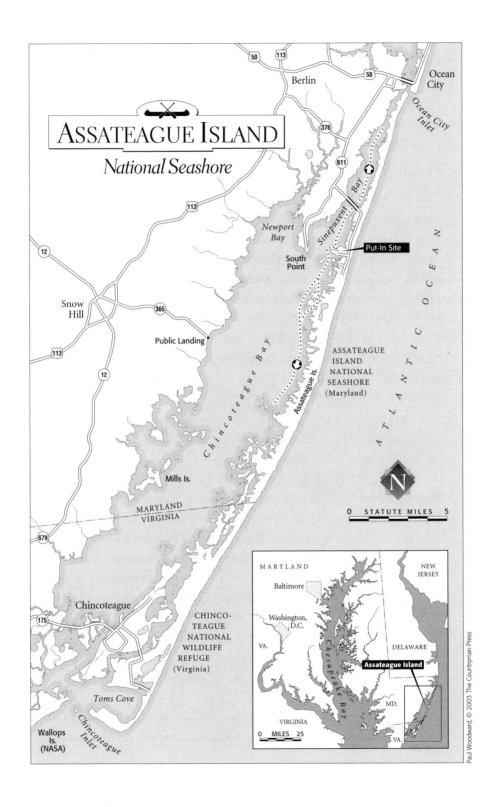

ASSATEAGUE ISLAND
National Seashore

50 113
Berlin
50
Ocean City
Ocean City Inlet

113
376
611

Sinepuxent Bay

12

Newport Bay

Put-In Site

South Point

Snow Hill

365

Public Landing

Chincoteague Bay

113

12

ASSATEAGUE ISLAND NATIONAL SEASHORE (Maryland)

A T L A N T I C   O C E A N

Assateague Is.

Mills Is.

MARYLAND
VIRGINIA

N

0   STATUTE MILES   5

679

Chincoteague

175

CHINCO-TEAGUE NATIONAL WILDLIFE REFUGE (Virginia)

Toms Cove

Wallops Is. (NASA)

Chincoteague Inlet

MARYLAND

NEW JERSEY

Baltimore

Washington, D.C.

VA.

DELAWARE

Chesapeake Bay

Assateague Island

MD.

VIRGINIA

VA.

0   MILES   25

Paddling here is often magical. There is nothing more spectacular than sitting in your kayak on a warm day with a slight breeze and basking in the serenity found observing one of Assateague's resident ponies munching on salt meadow hay.

Paddling Notes

One can paddle ½ hour or all day in Chincoteague and Sinepuxent bays. Up front you need to be concerned with three aspects of this area: first, a channel delineated by red and green channel markers exists out in the middle of the deeper section of the bays where powerboats zoom to and fro. Second, this area is notorious for its strong winds. There is a lot of fetch (open area for wind to travel and pick up speed) so it is easy to find yourself fighting against the wind when you are tired and trying to get back to the landing. Third, in the summer months, especially near the wooded areas of the island, mosquitoes rule. During this time of year stay on the edge of the marsh where there is a breeze and not much mosquito habitat.

That being said, Assateague Island paddling is spectacular. Start from the Old Ferry Landing and head out north or south depending on the wind prediction for the day.

Heading south you can paddle in and around numerous coves and islands. As the crow flies it is approximately a 14-mile paddle to the Maryland/Virginia border. Use the primitive bay side campgrounds as landmarks to keep your orientation. The first is Tingles Island campground 2 miles from Old Ferry Landing. (If you have an emergency there is a direct line to the ranger station near the beach area walking toward the Atlantic from the campsite.) Three miles further south you reach Pine Tree campground another 4½ miles and you reach Green Run campground. (Again, there are emergency phones near the beach as you walk from the campground.) In another 2½ miles you will find Pope Bay campground way up in the marsh. (No emergency phone here.)

Paddle around Tingles Island, get out and wade or swim in the water. It is often clear and the bottom hard for easy walking. Terrapins (see page 138) thrive in abundance here. If you see a small stick poking

2 to 3 inches above water and it disappears, you have just spotted one. Scan the liquid perimeter and realize disappearing sticks surround you.

Take time to hop onto the marsh of an island or one of the fingers of land pointing out from the shore. Stroll through fields of salt meadow hay searching for the shell of a blue crab that has shed or the remains of a blue heron's dinner. You will most likely see and paddle near the *WILD* ponies that inhabit Assateague Island. Enjoy them from a distance. *They have been known to kick and bite and you can receive a fine for getting too close. Do not feed them.* Just enjoy their presence and take pictures. They are very serene and beautiful to admire.

Paddling north from Old Ferry Landing, keep to the shore and pass under the bridge you crossed on your way in. This side takes you into Sinepuxent Bay. Islands and coves begin to diminish as you paddle north. It is still beautiful and usually there are fewer paddlers here. Once you pass under the causeway it is about 5 miles to the end of Assateague. However, we suggest staying well away from the tip of Assateague Island and Ocean City Inlet. There is a good deal of boat traffic and strong current that can suck you into the Atlantic if the tide is heading out.

The beauty of paddling this end of Assateague Island is that it is a short walk from Sinepuxent Bay to the Atlantic where you can relax on the beach and perhaps spot a group of porpoise passing by. There is much to admire on this stretch as you walk since it is almost all sand. Keep in mind that few people visit this end of Assateague because there is no road and it is a long hike from either the state or national parks. Keep a keen eye out for turtle eggs. Ask the folks at the ranger station what area of the beach to avoid at what time of year.

30. *Smith Island*

> **Length:** 7-8 mile round trip (includes spending time in Ewell) or as much paddling as you like.
> **Put-in Site:** Tylerton, Smith Island.
> **Driving Directions:** From Annapolis take US 50 east across the Chesapeake Bay Bridge through Salisbury. After passing through

Salisbury take US 13 south to Princess Anne. Continue on US 13 south past Princess Anne to MD 413 to Crisfield. From Crisfield take the Jason ferry to Tylerton, Smith Island.

Ferry Information: The ferry *Cap't Jason II* departs Crisfield for Tylerton at 12:30 and 5:00 PM and departs Tylerton at 7:00 AM and 3:30 PM to Crisfield daily. The fare is $20/person round trip. Make sure you are on the ferry to Tylerton. Your kayak can be transported on the roof of the ferry for an additional charge. Bring some straps and arrive early to arrange this. Parking is available at adjacent J.P. Tawes & Bro Hardware. For more information call: (410) 425-5931 or (410) 425-4471.

SMITH ISLAND is part of the archipelago just off the Eastern Shore of southern Maryland and northern Virginia. Between this chain of islands and the eastern shore is the famous Tangier Sound, a spectacular place to fish and cruise in a powerboat or sailboat and brimming with fascinating history, especially in regard to the seafood industry.

Around these islands lie some of the best habitat for soft- and hard-shell crabs. Of the four major islands that make up the chain, Bloodsworth Island, South Marsh Island, Smith Island, and Tangier Island (in Va.), only Smith and Tangier Island are still inhabited. Thus, Smith Island is the only inhabited island in Maryland accessible only by boat. Over time, erosion forced inhabitants to leave the other islands.

Smith Island was "discovered" by Captain John Smith when he explored the Chesapeake Bay in 1608. Of course, thousands of Native Americans inhabited the islands throughout pre-European discovery. English dissenters from Lord Baltimore's colony settled the island in 1657 and Smith Island is populated today by descendants of the original colonists (except for folks who own summer homes). The early settlers knew nothing about making a living off the water. They were mostly agrarian, and even put wooden "snowshoes" on their cattle to keep them from sinking as they grazed on salt meadow hay in the marsh.

Over time, however, "watermen" (this may not be "PC," but I have heard of only one or two women who have this career) of the area became famous for their ability to reap an astounding underwater har-

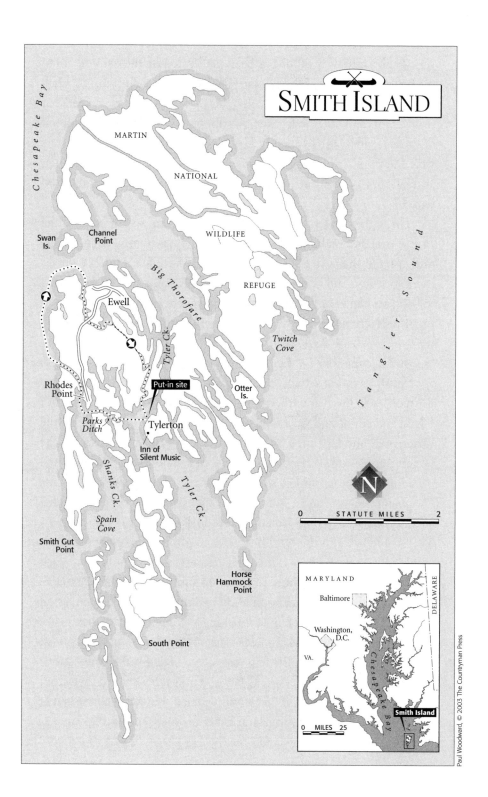

SMITH ISLAND

Chesapeake Bay

MARTIN

NATIONAL

Swan
Is.

Channel
Point

WILDLIFE

Big Thorofare

Ewell

REFUGE

*Twitch
Cove*

Tyler Ck.

Put-in site

Rhodes
Point

*Parks
Ditch*

Tylerton

Otter
Is.

Inn of
Silent Music

Shanks Ck.

Tyler Ck.

*Spain
Cove*

Smith Gut
Point

Horse
Hammock
Point

South Point

Tangier Sound

0   STATUTE MILES   2

N

MARYLAND

Baltimore

Washington,
D.C.

VA.

Chesapeake Bay

DELAWARE

Smith Island

0   MILES   25

vest. Their entire way of life has been predicated on the rise and fall of the seafood industry of the Chesapeake Bay. Hard-shell crabs, softshell crabs, oysters, eel, rockfish (striped bass), terrapin, croaker, speckled trout, clams and other delicacies contributed to the financial livelihood of the waterman and his family. For most watermen, crabs and oysters were the number one source of revenue. During the spring, summer, and fall they concentrate on harvesting crabs; during the winter, oysters.

Through over-harvesting, habitat destruction, and disease (in the case of oysters), making a living off the water has become increasingly difficult. For the past 20 years very few sons have followed in their fathers' footsteps and become watermen. Some have and they work hard to hang on. But each year gets tougher and there are increasing government restrictions on catch limits in an effort to allow the resource to make a comeback. As a result, many folks leave Smith Island for more "secure" occupations on the mainland.

Smith Island is actually made up of three separate islands with a town on each. Ewell and Rhodes Point are on the western side of Smith Island and connected via a road through the marsh. Tylerton is on the eastern side and separated from the other towns by water. Ewell has the largest population with stores, a couple of restaurants, and even some cars. Rhodes Point only has some residences. Tylerton has 70 residents (original residents) and a store, named the Drum Point Market, with a small diner. Due to their isolation Smith Islanders speak a specific dialect of English and use certain terms and phrases that only the locals would understand. There is no official government or police, but each town has a Methodist Church where community decisions are made.

Even with the original population dwindling, this is still a magical place and there are many families making a living from the Chesapeake Bay. The local economy is also receiving a boost due to tourism. A visit to Smith Island is worth the trip just to get a feel for the connections folks here have to the Chesapeake Bay and how it has shaped their lives. Just a little time here and you will find yourself somewhat connected as well. And as a bonus, Smith Island hosts the most spectacular sunsets and sunrises in all of Maryland.

Unloading the ferry Cap't Jason II *for a weekend of paddling and good eating at Smith Island*

Mike Savario

Paddling Notes

In a way this trip is more than a day trip due to the fact that you have to take the ferry to Smith Island and half the day is over by the time you get there. You need to spend the night in order to get in some good paddling since the last ferry from Tylerton to Crisfield is in the afternoon. But, it is worth the hassle and the time. The Inn of Silent Music is the only bed & breakfast in Tylerton, but it is an outstanding establishment with delicious breakfasts and dinners made from fresh local catch.

The ferry from Crisfield puts you off at the county dock in Tylerton. The county dock is not conducive to launching your kayak due to its height. If you are staying at the Inn of Silent Music there is an area near the bed & breakfast for launching. Or you may be able to use the launch spot on the Chesapeake Bay Foundation property (make sure to acquire permission). Either way you will need to carry your kayak some distance to the put-in. Sharryl or Leroy from the Inn will meet you at the dock with a cart for carrying your luggage, etc. If you have some wheels for you kayak you may want to bring them along.

After settling in you can spend a lazy afternoon just getting to know Tylerton by either walking around the town or paddling around the island of Tylerton. You could make the trip to Ewell, but why rush it. You will have already eaten lunch by now (which you can get at the Drum Point Market in Tylerton) and Sharryl and Leroy will be fixing you a fantastic dinner (make sure and ask them about this when you make your reservation; it is an additional cost). The paddling trip around Tylerton is about 3 miles. Or you can simply paddle south from the Inn of Silent Music into Tyler Creek and get a view of the bay. To paddle around Tylerton go left (south) from the inn and keep to the shore on your left. You will eventually come to a gut heading northwest that leads back to Tyler Creek north of the Inn. At the mouth of this gut turn left into Tyler Creek. The next opportunity to turn left will take you into the harbor, which is well worth exploring to see all the workboats and shanties used by the watermen.

As you exit the harbor and turn left into Tyler Creek you will pass the Chesapeake Bay Foundation (CBF) property. CBF conducts three-day environmental education trips for many Maryland students, CBF members, and others. You will also pass more shanties, docks, and boats

Heading out from the Inn of Silent Music B&B on a perfect day

Mike Savario

before you round the corner back to the Inn of Silent Music. Be careful to stay to the left side of Tyler Creek as you paddle. This is basically Tylerton's highway.

The next morning after an excellent breakfast get out on the water and head across Tyler Creek to what the locals call "refrigerator gut" (referring to the refrigerators that have been deposited there through the years) or the official name, Parks Ditch. This gut is west southwest from the Inn. Pass through the gut and you are in Shanks Creek. This is a pretty open area and can be quite shallow at low tide. Paddle north from here and pass Rhodes Point on your right. Continue on and you will enter the Chesapeake Bay via Sheep Pen Gut. On the left side of Sheep Pen Gut where it enters the bay is a good place for a break. Here you will have to decide if the conditions are conducive to open water paddling. If so head on out and paddle north along the shore to the next opportunity to paddle east into the channel that will take you to Ewell. Notice breakwaters at the entrance and channel markers. Again, keep to the right side away from powerboats. The area you just passed on your right is part of the Martin National Wildlife Refuge. The remainder of the island to the north is all part of the Martin National Wildlife Refuge.

Follow the channel markers into town. You will eventually pass a large shanty on the right. Just past this shanty and before the dock for the Ewell ferry turn right into a small harbor. Paddle straight and you will find a boat ramp to land your kayak. Put your boat off to the side to keep the landing clear while you stroll around town.

There are many places to visit in town. Now is the time to get that crab cake. My favorite place is Ruke's General Store and Seafood Deck just to the left of the boat landing and across the street from the Smith Island Center Museum. This is a small store small filled with all kinds of knickknacks. You can take a seat in the back, but order at the counter first. A rest room is available as well. There is also the Bayside Inn near the ferry dock.

Take some time to mosey around and observe life in Ewell. The pace may seem a little faster because there is enough room here to have a few cars so folks can travel back and forth from Rhodes Point. There is much to see and most folks will be glad to visit with you and answer questions. Be sure to check out the Smith Island Center Museum (410-425-3351; 1-800-521-9189). This small museum has permanent exhibits related to the history of the island, working on the water, and the interaction of people and the Chesapeake Bay.

After exploring Ewell you can make your way back to Tylerton. You will paddle out of the harbor and turn right into Levering Creek, which will lead you back to Tylerton. Keep paddling southeast past the end of Ewell. As you go keep to the right, away from boat traffic. There will be less boat traffic on your way back, but the occasional skiff could come flying through. As you go you will need to take your first left and then an immediate right to stay in this gut. Eventually Levering Creek will dogleg left, then right and then left again before it dumps you into the flats just west of Tylerton. From here just head southeast to the Inn of Silent Music in Tylerton (410-428-3541; www.innofsilentmusic. com). Now it is time to take a shower, relax on the porch and soon devour a scrumptious meal while watching the setting sun.

As with many of the trips described in this guide there are many

Blue Crabs *(Callinectes sapidus)*

Spring and summer are great times of the year to spot blue crabs feeding, swimming and burrowing in the sand. They possess several nicknames including Jimmy for males and Sook for females. The one I like the most is beautiful swimmers, which is the English translation of the blue crab's Latin name. Because of the paddle fins attached to the ends of the two appendages on the back of the body, blue crabs are able to swim sideways. The leading claw is tucked in while the trailing claw is extended in the opposite direction of travel trailing behind the body. Folks refer to this as "doing the Heisman," named after the shape of the Heisman trophy awarded each year to the best college football player. The blue crab has five pairs of appendages and uses three of them for crawling around scavenging on the bottom and escaping prey, the others for swimming and balance. And then there are the claws. The claws are used to tear prey apart, hold food, and bring food to the mouth. All of these appendages can be used to help the crab bury in the sand when it senses danger.

The top of the blue crab's shell is almost exactly the same color as Chesapeake Bay water. Therefore, they are hard to spot in any depth beyond 2 feet or so. Often they give themselves away by moving and you can follow them and observe their scavenging. They will eat almost anything dead or alive including their own kind when the unlucky crab is in the soft stage, having outgrown its shell and just molted. It takes about 24 hours for a crab's shell to harden. During a good deal of that time they are completely helpless and vulnerable. Their claws have none of the awesome pinching and puncturing power they possess when hard. Handling a blue crab in the soft stage is unique, sort of like rappelling off a cliff. Your body says this just is not right, but it is safe if all your gear is set up correctly. And it is safe to pet a huge blue crab when it is in the soft stage.

Interestingly enough, the only time crabs can mate is when the female is soft having just gone through her final molt. Search the pilings of piers in the area and you may notice what locals call a "doubler," two crabs together with one behind and on top of the other, its claws wrapped around in front. The crab on the inside is the female and the male is protecting her from predators until her shell is hard. Crabs mate from June through October and as soon as the female is pregnant she begins her migration directly to the mouth of the Chesapeake.

During the winter months the females burrow at the mouth of the bay where they hibernate until spring. The pregnant females have what is termed a "sponge," or mass of eggs, attached to their underbelly. From May through October females spawn young crabs that are tossed all about the ocean and eventually make their way back to the mouth of the

Chesapeake to start their trek up the bay and its tributaries. By the age of 12 to 16 months crabs have reached sexual maturity and an average size of 5 inches. As the weather grows cold all the females make their way back to the mouth of the Chesapeake and the males burrow in the mud wherever they happen to be at that time and overwinter.

Many times you can find the spent shell of a blue crab washed up on shore. Check to see if it is merely a dead crab or the former home of one. If it is empty and the back opens up easily you have found a spent shell. Turn it upside down and observe the "apron" or the unusual looking piece of shell rising from the bottom of the crab. If it looks like the Washington Monument you have found the former exoskeleton of a Jimmy or male crab. If it looks like a pyramid she was an immature crab or sook. If it looks like the Capitol Building she was mature.

Approach a crab and they will either scurry for cover, bury in the bottom, or raise their claws in defiance. Beware, their claws are very powerful and can inflict a good deal of pain. However, they are no match for great blue herons and other predators like sea gulls (depending on the crab and the relative size of the bird, of course). Check the scat of gulls and herons and you will find the ground-up remains of many a blue crab.

In the Chesapeake region steaming and eating blue crabs are considered a constitutional right. One cannot go a summer without joining friends around a picnic table covered with newspaper, crabs and Old Bay seasoning. If you do, it's been a bad summer and you need to get out more often. There is nothing sweeter than the smell of crabs steaming. Folks around here like to put a little water in a pot, add some Old Bay and perhaps some vinegar and lemon and steam the blue crab until it is bright red. When eating, one can add more Old Bay and perhaps do some butter dipping. The backfin of the blue crab is often considered the best, but I love all of it.

Softshell crabs are a delicacy around the Chesapeake area. Usually pan fried or sautéed, they are served as a main course or as a sandwich. Make sure you try one and also find a place that makes good crab cakes. Maryland crab cakes are the best. I can say that because I am from Louisiana where seafood rules. Keep in mind that hard crabs must be 5¼ inches wide from point to point and softshells 3½ inches from point to point to be legally harvested. If you eat in a place breaking the rules let them know.

Unfortunately, this rite of summer has come at a fairly steep price. Crabs are suffering due to over-harvesting and loss of habitat in the region. There are many concerned groups addressing the issue and trying to strike a balance between enjoying a natural resource and insuring its future survival. Still, it is nostalgic to watch a waterman picking up his pots (square wire mesh crab traps) and dumping his catch on board.

Watermen use flat bottom boats that draw very little water allowing the craft to get into shallow areas. Softshell crabs are usually caught with what is called a crab scrape. It is a rectangular device with a mesh net. The scrape is dragged behind the workboat through shallow waters where grasses grow (submerged aquatic vegetation). As the scrape skims the grasses it catches everything in its path. This includes softshell crab because they hide in the grasses until their shell is hard. If you ever get the chance to join a waterman as he pulls his pots or drags a scrape jump on it. You will see critters you have never seen before, especially when you go scraping. I have been fortunate enough to see sea horses, all kinds of small crabs, pipefish, worms, and entire ecosystems displayed on a clump of shell. *—M.S.*

more miles to paddle and places to discover around Smith Island. Take a look at your chart and make a plan for your day.

Note: If you own one, bring a VHF radio, which is the primary mode of electronic communication on Smith Island. Before departing on your kayak trip learn what channel the locals monitor. If you need help hail a waterman on this channel. They will be able to find you quicker than anyone else in the area. (It is also very interesting to listen to the traffic on the radio between the locals.)

Appendixes

APPENDIX A

Safety Resources

THE QUICKEST WAY to access help in a true emergency is to call 911 to activate the emergency response system—the operator can better, and more quickly determine what agency to dispatch to your rescue. Both the Natural Resources Police and the Coast Guard monitor VHF channel 16. What follows is the general contact information for the Maryland Natural Resources Police and the United States Coast Guard. You must dial the complete 10-digit number.

Maryland Natural Resources Police: A search and rescue, law enforcement, and fisheries agency with land, water, and air support. For general information visit www.dnr.state.md.us/nrp or for safety education courses call 410-260-3280.

 Statewide Emergency Number: 410-260-8888
 Lower Western Shore: 301-645-0062
 Central Western Shore: 410-974-5640
 Upper Western Shore: 410-356-7060
 Upper Eastern Shore: 410-758-2890
 Middle Eastern Shore: 410-820-1314
 Lower Eastern Shore: 410-548-7070

Maryland State Police: Depending on the region, the state police can provide some on-water aid, and can help facilitate and coordinate the emergency response system.

 St. Mary's County (Leonardtown, Barrack T): 301-884-8586

Charles County (La Plata, Barrack H): 301-392-1200

Calvert County (Prince Frederick, Barrack U): 410-535-1400

Prince George's County: (Forestville, Barrack L): 301-568-8101

Anne Arundel County (Annapolis, Barrack R): 410-268-6101

Harford County (Bel Air, Barrack D): 410-838-4101

Kent County (Chestertown, Division of Barrack S): 410-778-4511

Queen Anne's County (Centerville, Division of Barrack S): 410-758-1101

Talbot, Dorchester & Caroline Counties (Easton, Division of Barrack I): 410-822-3101

Worcester County (Berlin, Division of Barrack V): 410-641-3101

Somerset County (Princess Anne, Division of Barrack V): 443-260-3700

Cecil County (North East, MD, Division of Barrack F): 410-398-8101

Kent County (Chestertown, Division of Barrack S): 410-778-4511

Somerset County (Princess Anne, Division of Barrack V): 443-260-3700

United States Coast Guard: They provide a wide variety of services, many of which are described in their web site at www.uscg.mil. The Chesapeake Bay's Coast Guard stations are under the umbrella of the Atlantic group, and are based out of District 5's, Activities Baltimore. Their web site is www.uscg.mil/d5. The following are the numbers for the stations that would conduct search and rescue operations.

Atlantic Division Search and Rescue: 757-398-6390

Chesapeake Bay, District 5, Activities Baltimore main number: 410-576-2651

Small Boat Station St. Inigoes (St. Mary's County): 301-872-4344/45

Small Boat Station Annapolis: 410-267-8108

Small Boat Station Curtis Bay (Baltimore): 410-576-2625/8051

Appendix B

Preventing and Recognizing Hypothermia and Hyperthermia

THE MOST COMMON PADDLING INJURY is said to be shoulder related, specifically dislocations. These usually occur when the paddler strikes a hard surface with the paddle while having a firm grip and perhaps too high a stroke. The paddle stops and the shoulder can pop out. This injury could also happen during rolling or bracing or perhaps practicing some other skill. There usually has to be some force involved.

But the most common paddling "injuries" we see are sunburn and dehydration. Which brings us to two very serious temperature related "injuries" that, at least in the waters we describe in this guide, you are most likely to experience: hypothermia and hyperthermia.

Hypothermia occurs when the core body temperature drops below 98.6 degrees. In the Chesapeake Bay region our summers are usually quite hot and humid and the winters way too cold for casual paddling. Let's assume you will be paddling April through October. As we write this in early April the water at Thomas Point Lighthouse just south of Annapolis is only 49.8 degrees. Just the other day the air temperature was above 70 degrees. These conditions make spring the trickiest paddling season. Cabin fever rules and a beautiful day invokes the desire to get on the water. Let's say you are standing around in your shorts and T-shirt on this 70-degree day when a breeze kicks up or the sun becomes shrouded by clouds: you feel chilled. What you experience is called the "cold response." Blood flow to the skin is reduced in an attempt to lessen heat loss at the surface of your body. You may get "goose bumps" and begin to shiver, which is your body's way of trying to create heat through movement. You may also feel the need to urinate or what is called "cold diuresis." The more water your body holds onto the harder it has to work to keep that water warm, so it tries to get rid of it. This need to get rid of fluid can lead to dehydration.

If you stay in this environment long enough your core body temperature could drop and you would begin to experience mild hypothermia. If not treated, you would head into severe hypothermia. Hypothermia can occur gradually, or immediately if you were to capsize in your T-shirt and shorts on a day like today, with water this cold.

When your body begins to experience cold but your core temperature has remained normal and hasn't yet begun to cool, it shunts blood away from the extremities (hands, arms, legs, feet) and pools it around your vital organs (including your brain) to keep them warm. If your core temperature drops your motor skills and clarity of thought become inhibited. In wilderness first aid courses this condition is called the UMBLES because you stumble, fumble, and mumble. Your fingers no longer work and you may have trouble speaking clearly because the part of the brain that controls motor function and speech shuts down first in a "mild hypothermia" situation. Mild hypothermia is defined as a lowering of the core body temperature, but not below 90 degrees.

In cold water immersion this happens immediately. Often in water folks do not die of hypothermia; they usually drown first. The most common cause of drowning is the rapid loss of muscular coordination associated with hypothermia. No longer able to swim, the person sinks and inhales water. (Always wear your PFD.) Drowning can also happen instantly in such immersion due to the involuntary gasp that happens when your head hits cold water. This will immediately deprive you of any reserve air and limit your consciousness to a few seconds.

Always dress for the water temperature you would encounter if you were to capsize on the day you are paddling. A local shop here in Annapolis will not rent kayaks to customers who want to launch from their dock if the water is below 50 degrees unless they have a dry suit. A wet suit is necessary if the water is between 50 and 60 degrees.

If you plan to paddle on a day with 50 degree water temperature and 70 degree air temperature in the areas we describe in this guide, we would suggest, at the minimum, wearing a wetsuit with a dry top, neoprene socks with neoprene booties, some type of hood (either neoprene or fleece lined rubber), and neoprene gloves. You will certainly warm up as you paddle, so you can regulate your heat by taking off the cap and gloves and play it safe by paddling in water that is very shallow and stay very close to shore.

Always wear your PFD. This will help you retain heat and keep you afloat if something goes wrong. If you get too hot, land your boat and take a break and stretch your legs. You could even wade in if super hot. Your best bet would be to wear a dry suit with insulation inside; the above head, hand, and foot gear; and to get out of your kayak every now and then and wade in the water, from shore, if you get too hot.

We don't discuss how to treat hypothermia in this book, but suggest that you take a wilderness first aid course (see appendix), a wilderness advanced first aid course, or a wilderness first responder course. To quote the *Outward Bound Wilderness First-Aid Handbook,* "mild hypothermia is an urgent field problem. Unless positive changes occur,... severe hypothermia will soon follow." Prevention is key. Don't let it sneak up on you.

Hyperthermia is an increase in core body temperature. Move forward to July or August when temperatures are in the 90s with a heat index of 101 degrees thanks to massive humidity. This is one hot, oppressive day. But, still, you just have to paddle. The last thing you want to do is wear your PFD, but always wear it anyway.

Today dressing in a T-shirt and shorts would not be a problem. Of course, many folks like to wear high-tech, wicking clothing which is fine. The key today is to stay hydrated and to not overexert.

Just as there is a "cold response" in hypothermia there is a "heat response" in hyperthermia. Instead of limiting the flow of blood to your extremities the blood vessels of your skin are dilating, allowing heat to flow to the surface to produce sweat. As the sweat evaporates you cool down. If there is too much humidity the sweat cannot evaporate (and no cooling takes place) but you are losing a ton of water.

During "heat response" you are still a normal, clear-headed kayaker. Your body temperature is normal. You are shedding layers, drinking water, and perhaps taking a break in the shade. You are stopping the physical activity that is causing your body to work so hard to keep your temperature normal. Your common sense is in intact.

Heat exhaustion can occur if you continue the activity and do not drink enough fluids. On such a humid day you can drink fluids all you like, but if sweat is just pouring out and not evaporating because of high humidity you are merely becoming dehydrated and not cooling down a bit. You have to stop your activity even though your body temperature is still fine. If you do not, you will become dehydrated and may begin to experience increased respiration and pulse rate. You will still be thinking clearly, but you may feel weak, very thirsty, and nauseated. Vomiting is common at the heat exhaustion stage.

The next stage is heat stroke. Your body temperature will be above 105 degrees and you are now dealing with a life-threatening emergency requiring immediate treatment.

Again, prevention is the key. Make sure you eat a good meal before you go and drink plenty of fluids. Food usually has all the salts you need to deal with heavy sweating. Sports drinks are fine but not necessary, and salt tablets are completely unnecessary. Dress for the day. Wear protective clothing if necessary. We often wear a long-sleeved, lightweight shirt to keep from burning our skin or apply sunscreen on the way to the paddle (best to put it on before unloading your boat, gives you all day protection and your hands are clean enough to rub into your face). Reapply sunscreen throughout the day. Put sunscreen on your face, hands, neck, legs, and feet. Wear a wide brimmed hat that covers most of your face and the back of your neck.

Drink water the moment you awake and all day long. Just put a filled plastic gallon jug behind your seat or elsewhere and refill your water bottle as often as necessary. Keep in mind your body needs water before you feel thirsty. Carry snacks and other food appropriate to the amount of time you are paddling. And, before you get too hot, take the steps necessary to cool down. Stop the activity, sit in the shade, re-hydrate, and perhaps take a swim.

Education is the key to prevention. Check out these web sites to find course dates in your area: www.wildmed.com and Solo: www.solo-schools.com.

Appendix C

Accommodations and Tourism Information

HERE ARE THE TOP RESOURCES for tourism information and accommodations. Rather than distill what each county tourism agency provides, we include the main contact information for each county's visitor center. Besides providing information about hotels, most tourism web sites also contain information about the area's natural and cultural history, and many were useful in researching this book. We have organized the following information in the same geographical order as the book, loosely grouping trips by regions and counties. Kayak rental locations have also been included in this section. Remember, Maryland is small and most areas of the state are within a two-hour drive of one another.

Statewide Accommodations Resources

Maryland Office of Tourism: A clearinghouse of information on hotels, bed & breakfasts, camping, and links to other tourism sites. They can be contacted at www.mdisfun.org or 1-800-MDISFUN (634-7386).

Maryland Department of Natural Resources (DNR): The primary state agency that protects Maryland's natural resources and the source for state park information or reservations. DNR Resources Planning develops plans for water trails wholly or largely within DNR lands. For general information, they can be contacted at www.dnr.state.md.us or

1-877-620-8367. For reservations, visit www.reservations.dnr. state.md.us or call 1-888-432-2267. The DNR also sponsors a Nature Tourism Program to create opportunities to explore Maryland's remote and scenic areas: 410-968-1565.

Maryland Bed & Breakfast Association: A resource that is only accessible via the internet, but provides a thorough registry of all of Maryland's bed & breakfasts, along with their phone numbers and/or web sites. They can be contacted at www.marylandbb.com.

Maryland Greenways Commission: 410-260-8780 or www.dnr. state.md.us/greenways.

www.BayDreaming.com: A Chesapeake Bay area tourism directory that provides weather, tides and history information along with hotels and bed & breakfasts.

Area Specific Resources

These resources have been organized in the same order as the trip descriptions, and have been further grouped by region and county.

Western Shore

Southern Maryland: St. George's Island, McIntosh Run, Allen's Fresh Run, Mattawoman Creek, Parker Creek, and Chesapeake Beach trips

St. Mary's County: (St. George's Island and McIntosh Run) For the St. Mary's County Visitor's Center contact www.co.saint-marys.md.us or call 1-800-327-9023. There are plenty of bed & breakfasts in St. Mary's City and Solomon's Island. The local tourism web site for Leanordtown is www.leonardtown.net. Camp Merryelande Vacation Cottages on St. George's Island has cabins, tent sites, and RV hookups in their location on St. George's Island. Their number is 1-800-382-1073 and their web site is www.campmd.com.

Charles County: (Allen's Fresh Run and Mattawoman Creek) For the Charles County Visitor's Center, call 1-800-SOMDFUN, 301-645-0558 or go to www.explorecharlescomd.com. There are a few hotels in

Indian Head, with plenty more hotels in La Plata and Waldorf. Smaller bed & breakfasts can found in the countryside away from these large towns. On the Mattawoman Creek, camping is available at Smallwood State Park. For reservations and information contact Maryland DNR at the number and web site given in Statewide resources above.

Calvert County: (Parker Creek and Chesapeake Beach) For the Calvert County Visitor's Center, call 301-812-1046 or visit www.co. cal.md.us. Prince Frederick and Chesapeake Beach both have hotels and bed & breakfasts. Cottage camping is available at Breezy Point by the week, month, and season; visit www.chesapeake.net/breezypointma-rina or call 410-535-4356 for more information.

Central Maryland: Mattaponi Creek, Western Branch, Upper Patuxent, Spa Creek to South River, and Annapolis trips

Prince George's County: Visit www.goprincegeorgescounty.com or call 1-888-925-8300 for the visitor's center. There are several hotels around Upper Marlboro and Bowie, and there are primitive campsites available by reservation only at Patuxent River Park for groups up to 200 people. There is also a kayak/canoe accessible site at the park, suitable for small groups. Camping is $4 per person per night, or $3 per person if you are a Prince Georges or Montgomery County resident. For information call 301-627-6074. Cedarville State Forest is at the southern edge of the county, about 20 minutes from Patuxent River Park, and is a multiple site family campground with bathrooms and shower facilities. For reservations and information contact Maryland DNR at the number and web site given in Statewide resources.

Anne Arundel County: Contact the visitor's center by visiting www.visit-annapolis.org or by calling 410-280-0445. There are multiple hotels and a large number of bed & breakfasts in Annapolis—this is a popular tourist destination, so make sure to reserve ahead. Springriver Corporation is a kayak retailer and rental shop for both on-site and car-top rentals. They are located at 311 Severn Avenue in Eastport and can be called at 410-263-2303. They have three other locations in Balti-more, Rockville and Falls Church. Eastern Mountain Sports is a retail chain that offers kayak rentals for car-top rentals only (no water access from shop). Call 410-573-1240. Amphibious Horizons Sea Kayaking is a kayak guide company that offers rentals and kayak instruction from Quiet Waters Park in Annapolis as well as day, camping, and bed-and-breakfast trips to more than 30 Chesapeake Bay destinations. Visit www.amphibioushorizons.com or call 1-888-I-LUV-SUN or 410-267-8742.

Upper Bay: Gunpowder Falls, Susquehanna River trips

Baltimore City: (Gunpowder Falls) Call 1-877-BALTIMORE or visit www.baltimore.org. There are numerous hotels in the popular downtown harbor area of the city.

   Harford County: (Gunpowder Falls, Susquehanna River) Call 1-800-597-2649 or visit www.harfordmd.com. The nearest camping facilities for the Gunpowder are the two cabins at the Hammerman Area of Gunpowder State Park. Various hotels are strung along US 40 and I-95. Havre De Grace offers dozens of hotels and bed & breakfasts, and the definitive source for information is the Havre de Grace Office of Tourism & Visitor Center. They can be contacted at 1-800-851-7756 or www.hdgtourism.com. The best camping in the area is in Susquehanna River State Park. Contact Maryland DNR (see Statewide resources above) for reservations or information about either the Gunpowder or Susquehanna State Park.

Eastern Shore

Upper Eastern Shore: Perryville, Upper Sassafras, Sassafras,
Chester River, and Eastern Neck Wildlife Refuge trips

Cecil County: (Perryville) For Cecil County Tourism, www.seececil.org. For camping at Elk Neck State Park, contact Maryland DNR (see general resources).

   Kent County: (Upper Sassafras, Sassafras, Chester River, Eastern Neck) Visit www.kentcounty.com or call 410-778-0416. There are a few hotels, and bed & breakfasts abound in the area. There are no state campgrounds in the county. For Chestertown tourism, visit www.Chestertown.com. For Eastern Neck Island see the U.S. Fish and

Wildlife Service web page at www.easternneck.fws.org or call 410-639-7056.

Prospect Bay, Tuckahoe Creek, Wye Island, Tilghman Island, and Oxford/Tred Avon trips

Queen Anne County, Talbot County and Caroline County: (Prospect Bay, Tuckahoe Creek, Wye Island NRMA, Tilghman, Oxford/Tred Avon): See Queen Anne County Tourism: www.qac.org; click "Business and Tourism" at the top of the page.

Caroline County: www.carolinemd.org ; click "Caroline Tourism" on the left of the page. For Tuckahoe Creek State Park Reservations see www.reservations.dnr.state.md.us or 888-432-CAMP. Contact the park directly: 410-820-1668, or for State Forest and Park Service general information: 1-800-830-3974. For more detailed information on the Tuckahoe Creek history and culture visit The Old Harford Town Maritime Center located at 10215 River Landing Road, Denton, MD 21629, 410-241-8661 or see their web site: www.riverheritage.org. You can obtain a *Choptank & Tuckahoe Rivers Water Trail* map full of history, culture and points of interest along your paddle. Accommodations: www.dnr.stat.md.us. Maryland Department of Natural Resources web site; www.reservations.dnr.state.md.us.

Talbot County: For Wye Island see the Talbot County Government web site: www.talbgov.org and the Talbot County Recreation and Parks: 410-822-2955. See the Department of Natural Resources for general information on Wye Island: www.dnr.state.md.us. Camping on Wye Island is permitted for groups only. To contact the Wye Island office directly call: 410-827-7577. For Tilghman Island see the Talbot County Government web site above and www.tilghmanisland.com. For Oxford/Tred Avon see the Talbot County Government web site above as well as: www.baydreaming.com/oxford.htm and www.riverheritage.org/Riverguide/Trip/html/a_landing_at_oxford.html.

Taylor's Island, Blackwater National Wildlife Refuge, and Transquaking River Loop Trail trips

Dorchester County: See www.tourdorchester.org. For Taylor's Island WMA see: www.dnr.state.md.us/publiclands/eastern/taylorisland.html

or call the Lecompe Wildlife Office: 410-376-3236. For Blackwater NWR see the U.S. Fish and Wildlife Service: www.blackwater.fws.gov. Also see the Friends of Blackwater at: www.friendsofblackwater.org. Access if available to a camera mounted on an active osprey nest. Or call the refuge at: 410-228-2677. For the Transquaking River Loop Trail see the Fishing Bay WMA web page: www.dnr.state.md.us/publiclands/eastern/fishingbay.html and the Maryland Greenways Commission: 410-260-8780 or www.dnr.state.md.us/greenways.

Pocomoke River/Nassawango Creek, Janes Island, Assateague Island, and Smith Island trips

Worcester County: (Pocomoke/Nassawango Creek, Assateague) For Worcester County Tourism see: www.visitworcester.org and the Maryland Greenways Commission: 410-260-8780 or www.dnr.state.md.us/greenways. For Pocomoke State Park at Shad Landing see: www.reservations.dnr.state.md.us or call 800-432-CAMP. For Assateague Island National Seashore information see the National Park Service web site: www.nps.gov or call the National Park office: 410-641-3030. The National Park has primitive campsites with pit toilets. For Assateague Island State Park information see www.dnr.state.md.us/publiclands/eastern/assateague.html. For camping reservations see: www.reservations.dnr.state.md.us or call: 800-432-CAMP. The State Park has hot showers and "real" bathrooms.

Somerset County (Janes Island Water Trail and Smith Island): See www.visitsomerset.com. Smith Island Accommodations: The Inn of Silent Music, Tylerton: 410-428-3541; www.innofsilentmusic.com. Smith Island Motel, Ewell: 410-968-1110. Ewell Tide Inn Bed and Breakfast: 410-425-2141. Smith Island Getaway, Ewell: 410-425-3541. For reservations at Janes Island State Park: 1-888-432-CAMP or www.reservations.dnr.state.md.us or to reach the park directly: 410-968-1565.

APPENDIX D: *Beaufort Wind Scale*

This scale was developed in the early 1800s for frigate ships.
The effects on the water can differ according to your paddling location.

Beaufort Number	Wind Speed (knots)	Wind Description	Water Description
No force	0 knots	calm	flat calm
1	1–3	light air	ripples
2	4–6	light breeze	small wavelets
3	7–10	gentle breeze	scattered white-caps and large wavelets
4	11–16	moderate breeze	lots of whitecaps; small waves lengthen
5	17–21	fresh breeze	mostly whitecaps with spray: moderate waves Small Craft Advisory Issued
6	22–27	strong breeze	whitecaps everywhere; more spray
7	28–33	near gale	foam from waves begins blowing in streaks; sea heaps up
8	34–40	gale	foam is blown in well defined streaks; crests begin breaking Gale Warning Issued
9	41–47	strong gale	dense streaking; spray reduces visibility
10	48–55	whole gale	sea begins to roll and look white Storm Warning Issued
11	56–63	violent storm	sea covered with white foam patches; large waves
12	64+	hurricane	air filled with foam and spray; almost no visibility

Land
Description

nothing stirring

smoke drifts gently according to wind direction

air movement can be felt on your face

leaves and twigs in motion

loose paper blows around; small branches move

flags ripple: small trees
begin to sway

large trees and branches move; whistling heard
in sailboat rigging

whole tree sways

branches and twigs torn from trees, trouble
making headway on foot

roof shingles peeled from houses

trees uprooted; structural damage to buildings

widespread damage

major, widespread damage

Resources

MANY OF THE FOLLOWING RESOURCES were consulted in the writing of this book. An asterisk (*) marks any book that is a portable and concise addition to your on-water natural history library. An exclamation point (!) marks a book that we recommend for your home library. Web sites and recommended magazines are also listed.

Field Guides and Natural History Resources

Bull & Farrand, Jr. *The Audubon Society Field Guide to North American Birds, Eastern Region.* New York: Knopf, 1977, Tenth printing: 1983.

Burns, Jasper. *Fossil Collecting in the Mid-Atlantic States.* Baltimore: John's Hopkins University Press, 1991.

Forey, Pamela and Fitzsimons, Cecilia. *An Instant Guide to Reptiles and Amphibians.* Longmeadow Press, Atlantis Publications Ltd., 1987.

Horton, Tom. *An Island Out of Time.* New York: W. W. Norton and Company, Inc., 1996.

! Horton, Tom. *Bay Country: Reflections on the Chesapeake.* New York: Ticknor & Fields, 1987.

Horton, Tom. *Turning the Tide: Saving the Chesapeake Bay.* Washington, D.C.: Island Press, 1991.

* Hurley, Linda M. *Field Guide to the Submerged Aquatic Vegetation of Chesapeake Bay.* Annapolis, MD: U.S. Fish and Wildlife Service, 1992.

Kenny, Hammil. *Place Names of Maryland, Their Origin and Meaning.* Waverly, 1961.

* Little, Elbert L. *The Audubon Society Field Guide to North American Trees: Eastern Region.* New York: Alfred A. Knopf, 1980.

! Lippson, Alice and Robert Lippson. *Life in the Chesapeake Bay.* Baltimore: Johns Hopkins University Press, 1984.

Meanley, Brooke. *Birds and Marshes of the Chesapeake Bay Country.* Centreville, MD: Tidewater Publishers, 1975.

Meanley, Brooke. *The Patuxent River Wild Rice Marsh.* The Maryland-National Capital Park and Planning Commission, 1996.

! Murdy, Edward, Ray Birdsong and John Musick. *Fishes of the Chesapeake Bay.* Washington, D.C.: Smithsonian Institution Press, 1997.

*Peterson, Roger Tory. *A Field Guide to the Birds East of the Rockies.* 4th ed. Boston, MA: Houghton Mifflin Company, 1980.

Reshetiloff, Kathryn, ed. *Chesapeake Bay: Introduction to an Ecosystem.* Washington, D.C.: U.S. Environmental Protection Agency, 1995.

Ruthven, John A. and William Zimmerman. *Top Flight: Speed Index to Waterfowl of North America.* 8th ed. Milwaukee, WI: Moebius Printing Company, 1979.

Shomette, Donald G. *Tidewater Time Capsule: History Beneath the Patuxent.* Centreville, MD: Tidewater Publishers, 1995.

Sibley, David Allen. *The Sibley Guide to Bird Life & Behavior.* New York: Alfred A. Knopf, 2001.

*Silberhorn, Gene M. *Common Plants of the Mid-Atlantic Coast: A Field Guide.* Baltimore: Johns Hopkins University Press, 1999.

Webster, Wm. David, James F. Parnell and Walter C. Biggs, Jr. *Mammals of the Carolinas, Virginia and Maryland.* Chapel Hill: University of North Carolina Press, 1985.

*White, Christopher. *Chesapeake Bay: A Field Guide.* Centreville, MD: Tidewater Publishers, 1989.

! Williams, John Page. *Chesapeake Almanac: Following the Bay through the Seasons.* Centreville, MD: Tidewater Publishers, 1993.

www.acltweb.org (American Chestnut Land Trust: founded in 1986 to preserve the natural lands of Calvert County, particularly those in the watershed of Parkers Creek and Governors Run)

www.calvertmarinemuseum.org (Located in Solomon's Island, their museum and web site are a wealth of natural and historical information about the bay)

www.cbf.org (Chesapeake Bay Foundation: the largest organization dedicated solely to protect and preserve the Chesapeake Bay)

www.chesapeakebay.net (The Chesapeake Bay Program: a multistate alliance of agencies working to preserve and protect the bay)

www.cheslights.org (The website for the Chesapeake Chapter of the United States Lighthouse Society)

www.dnr.state.md.us (Department of Natural Resources: provides excellent links to a variety of environmental sites and is a clearinghouse of information about the natural resources of Maryland)

www.sentinelpublications.com/screwpile.htm (Online article about the origin of Screwpile lighthouses by Elinor DeWire, originally published by *Mariner's Weather Log*, Fall 1995)

Pamphlets

Chesapeake Gateways Network

National Park Service, 410 Severn Avenue, Suite 109, Annapolis, MD 21403: www.baygateways.net or 1-866-BAYWAYS for a map/guide.

The Pocomoke River Greenway, prepared for The Maryland Greenways Commission by Greenways and Resource Planning, Maryland Department of Natural Resources.

Wye Island Natural Resources Management Area: State Forest and Park Service, pamphlet: 410-260-8888.

Maryland Guidebooks

Adkins, Leonard. *Maryland: An Explorer's Guide.* Woodstock, VT: The Countryman Press, 2002.

Anderson, Elizabeth B. *Annapolis: A Walk Through History.* Centreville, MD: Tidewater Publishers, 1984.

Blake, Allison. *The Chesapeake Bay Book: A Complete Guide.* 5th ed. Lee, MA: Berkshire House, 2002.

Colbert, Judy. *Maryland and Delaware: Off the Beaten Path.* 5th ed. Guilford, CT: Globe Pequot Press, 2001.

Gertler, Edward. *Maryland and Delaware Canoe Trails.* 3rd ed. Seneca, MD: Seneca Press, 1993

Venn, Tamsin. *Sea Kayaking Along the Mid-Atlantic Coast: Coastal Paddling Adventures from New York to Chesapeake Bay.* Boston: Appalachian Mountain Club, 1994.

Williams, John Paige. *Exploring the Chesapeake in Small Boats.* Centreville, MD: Tidewater Publishers, 1992.

www.themre.org (Maritime Republic of Eastport's official web site with history and Eastport business information)

Maps

The Chesapeake Bay Chartbook: Maryland and Virginia. Alexandria, VA: Alexandria Drafting Company (ADC), 2001.

Guide to Cruising Maryland Waters. 15th ed. Annapolis, MD: Department of Natural Resources, 1990.

Maryland/Delaware Atlas and Gazetteer, DeLorme, P.O. Box 298, Freeport, ME 04032, (207) 865-4171, www.delorme.com.

Mid-Patuxent Estuarine Ecosystem Map. North Beach,MD: David Linthicum & Peggy Dickinson, 1995.

Topo! San Francisco: National Geographic Holdings, Inc., 2000.

ADC The Map People, Street Map Books for the appropriate county. Available from the Langenscheidt Publishing Group. Found in Barnes and Noble or convenience stores in the area. Or call ADC: 1-800-ADC-MAPS or see www.adcmap.com.

Sea Kayaking Books

! Broze, Matt and George Gronseth. *Sea Kayaker's Deep Trouble: True Stories and Their Lessons from Sea Kayaker Magazine.* Camden, ME:

Ragged Mountain Press, 1997.

! Burch, David. *Fundamentals of Kayak Navigation.* 3rd ed. Guilford, CT: Globe Pequot, 1999.

Foster, Nigel. *Nigel Foster's Sea Kayaking.* 2nd ed. Old Saybrook, CT: Globe Pequot, 1997.

Hutchinson, Derek. *The Complete Book of Sea Kayaking.* 4th ed. Old Saybrook, CT: Globe Pequot, 1995.

! Johnson, Shelley. *The Complete Sea Kayaker's Handbook.* Camden, ME: Ragged Mountain Press, 2002.

Lull, John. *Sea Kayaking Safety and Rescue.* Berkeley, CA: Wilderness Press, 2001.

Schumann, Roger and Jan Shriner. *Sea Kayak Rescue: The Definitive Guide to Modern Reentry and Recovery Techniques.* Guilford, CT: Globe Pequot, 2001.

Sea Kayaking Magazines

Atlantic Coastal Kayaker: PO Box 520, Ipswich, MA 01938.

Canoe and Kayak: www.canoekayak.com, P.O. Box 3146, Kirkland, WA 98083.

Paddler: www.paddlermagazine.com, P.O. Box 775450, Steamboat Springs, CO 80477.

Sea Kayaker: www.seakayakermag.com, P.O. Box 17029, Seattle, WA 98107.

Industry Resources

www.cpakayaker.com (Chesapeake Paddler's Association: bay-wide club that has six weekly paddling groups, organizes paddling trips and provides member-to-member instruction.)

www.acanet.org (American Canoe Association: a national paddle sport organization that fights for waterway conservation and access rights, as well as providing safety education, standards and instructor certification.)

www.bcu.org.uk (British Canoe Union: an England based organization with an international instructor and kayaker training and evaluative certifications.)

Wilderness Medicine and Outdoor Ethics

Hampton, Bruce and David Cole. *Soft Paths.* Harrisburg, PA: Stackpole Books, 1988.

Issac, Jeff and Peter Goth. *The Outward Bound Wilderness First Aid Handbook.* New York: Lyons & Burford, 1991.

www.wildmed.com. (Wilderness Medical Associates. A Maine based medical organization that provides Wilderness First Aid, First-Responder and Wilderness EMT certifications around the world.)

Wilderness Medical First Aid Training

National Outdoor Leadership Schools (NOLS): www.nols.edu

Wilderness Medical Associates: www.wildmed.com

Solo Schools: www.soloschools.com

Weather and Tide

*Lehr, Paul, R. Will Burnett and Herbert S. Zim, Ph.D, Sc.D. *The Golden Guide to Weather.* New York: Golden Press, 1987.

www.weather.gov (National Weather Service)

www.noaa.gov (National Oceanic and Atmospheric Administration, NOAA)

www.weather.com (The Weather Channel)

www.cbos.org (Chesapeake Bay Observing System, CBOS)

Index